THE REFERENCE SHELF *(Continued)*

Volume 23

No.
2. Representative American Speeches: 1950-1951. A. C. Baird. $1.75.

Volume 22

No.
3. Representative American Speeches: 1949-1950. A. C. Baird. $1.75.

Volume 20

No.
5. Federal World Government. J. E. Johnsen. $1.50.

Volume 19

No.
3. Free Medical Care. C. A. Peters. $1.25.

Volume 18

No.
3. Representative American Speeches: 1944-1945. A. C. Baird. $1.25.

No.
6. Palestine: Jewish Homeland? J. E. Johnsen. $1.25.

Volume 17

No.
4. Representative American Speeches: 1943-1944. A. C. Baird. $1.25.

Volume 16

No.
1. Representative American Speeches: 1941-1942. A. C. Baird. $1.25.

No.
6. Representative American Speeches: 1942-1943. A. C. Baird. $1.25.

THE REFERENCE SHELF

Vol. 29   No. 4

AMERICAN INDIANS

Compiled by
WALTER M. DANIELS

THE H. W. WILSON COMPANY
NEW YORK   1957

E
77
D3

PREFACE

The status of the American Indian in the United States is a perennial [ng-lasting] subject for debate. The issues involved have been raised most recently by the retreat under the Truman Administration from the liberal and cooperative policies of the Roosevelt Administration and by the efforts made under the Eisenhower Administration to "get the Government out of the Indian business."

The white man's treatment of the aboriginal inhabitants of North America has run a full cycle since the advent of the first European settlers. While the Spaniards sought to absorb the Indians and their culture, the Dutch and English followed policies of extermination and isolation. This trend was followed in the earliest days of the United States, when Indian affairs came under the jurisdiction of the War Department. With the transfer of these functions to the Department of the Interior in the late 1840's, there came an era of paternalism, marked by efforts to assimilate the Indians into our European type of culture by breaking up their reservations and alloting their lands to individual members of the tribes.

It became apparent, however, that something more than land ownership was needed to adapt the Indian to the white man's civilization. It was during the Civil War that President Lincoln said: "If we get through this war, and I live, this Indian system shall be reformed." It was not until the Hoover Administration, however, that the foundation was laid for such reform. A report made in 1928 by Lewis Meriam and his associates in the Institute for Government Research provided the basis for the new policies of three successive commissioners of Indian Affairs who sought conscientiously to reconcile the interests of the Indian and the white man.

The reform movement reached its high point in the Indian Reorganization Act of 1934, pushed through a none-too-willing Congress by Commissioner John Collier. The Act gave the Indians the greatest measure of control over their tribal affairs and lands that they had ever enjoyed under United States jurisdiction.

Collier's policies were abruptly reversed by his successor, Dillon S. Myer, an appointee of President Truman. The Indian Bureau reverted to paternalistic domination of Indian affairs. The main trend of policy under the Eisenhower Administration has been to reduce the Government's long-term involvement in Indian affairs by encouraging Indians to leave their reservations, sell their holdings, and "join the mainstream of American life."

All discussions of the status of American Indians resolve themselves at some point into the question: Shall the Indians be forcibly adapted to our European type of civilization, or shall they be gradually assimilated by a commingling of the best elements of our culture and theirs? The consensus of anthropologists, as reported in "Outlook for the Indians" in Section II of this book, is that the Indians will subsist indefinitely as "cultural islands," despite any attempt to swallow them up in the general population.

The cultural background of the Indians and the history of their relations with the white man are presented in the first two sections of this book. Section III reviews their legal status in our political system. Attempts to assimilate the Indians by turning over reservation jurisdiction to the states and by finding jobs and homes for Indian families in industrial centers are discussed in Sections IV and V. Section VI presents the programs of

Indian and non-Indian groups for long-range solution of the problems involved in Indian-white relations.

The editor wishes to express his appreciation to publishers and authors who have permitted the reproduction of materials in this volume. He is especially grateful to the Association on American Indian Affairs, the National Congress of American Indians, and the American Friends Service Committee for guidance and assistance in assembling material.

WALTER M. DANIELS

March 15, 1957

CONTENTS

I. INDIAN CULTURE

EDITOR'S INTRODUCTION

An identification of the American Indian—who he is and how he lives—leads off this section. It is followed by an article dispelling myths that have grown up about the Indian in the white man's history and literature.

An Indian organization director next defines the role of culture in determining behavior patterns, with special concern for its effects on efforts to assimilate the Indian into a European type of civilization. A free-lance writer recalls some of the Indian leaders who have made significant contributions to our national life.

The final article of this section calls attention to the influence of the Indians on white settlers of this continent and the Indians' contributions to our culture in the fields of politics, sociology, medicine, agriculture, and sports.

WHO ARE THE AMERICAN INDIANS? [1]

When Indians leave their reservations, when they intermingle with a predominantly white population and adapt their lives to its ways and customs, it becomes difficult sometimes to tell who are Indians and who are not. In counting Indians the Bureau of the Census has mainly depended upon whether or not the neighbors recognize a person as an Indian. The United States Indian Service, on the other hand, prefers to use a biological definition in terms of the degree of Indian ancestry

[1] From "This Is the Indian American," pamphlet by Louisa R. Shotwell, assistant secretary, Division of Home Missions, National Council of Churches of Christ in the United States of America. Friendship Press. 257 Fourth Avenue. New York 10. 1956. p3-16, 19-32. Reprinted by permission.

a person has. It is common practice today to consider anyone an Indian who has one-quarter Indian heritage.

Probably the most reasonable working definition for us is this: An Indian is somebody of Indian descent who continues to think of himself as an Indian and whom the community thinks of as Indian. . . .

Indian family life is rich and rewarding. Uncles, cousins, aunts, grandparents are near and well known. The child grows up in an easy atmosphere of belonging and being at home. The index of white twentieth century family pattern, the baby sitter, has no place on reservations. Where the family goes, the child goes, too.

On some reservations there is a saying that there are never any orphans. As soon as a child loses his parents, there is always a family ready to take in one more, and the new member comes as a real son or daughter. . . .

Another trait common to many Indians [is] the ability to work together as a group. Indeed, three centuries before Iroquois Indian steel workers helped to build a home for the United Nations on Manhattan Island's East Side, their ancestors in upstate New York developed a miniature united nations of their own. The old Iroquois Confederation of the Six Nations for many years kept Senecas, Cayugas, Onondagas, Oneidas, Mohawks, and Tuscaroras living peacefully side by side.

In 1934 Congress passed the Indian Reorganization Act, granting tribes authority to become incorporated for purposes of governing themselves and engaging in commercial enterprises. Fourteen years later the Hoover Commission Task Force on Indian Affairs commended Indian tribal organizations for their progress in the democratic handling of their own affairs. . . .

Indians know how to work together.

Again and again reports of teachers in mission schools ring variations on the theme: "Our students work well as part of a group." And then they add, "But they need continual encouragement to take initiative."

Indians are often very shy. . . . Yet among themselves or among old friends, Indians are completely natural. They have fun together and give way to both laughter and tears. The stolidity so often associated with them is a mask they use to cloak a feeling of insecurity in strange or hostile surroundings.

Many Indians are gifted with great manual dexterity, and they are careful and painstaking workmen. They are practical minded, quick to learn, if they see a real use for knowledge, indifferent if they see no reason for it.

Their natural tempo is deliberate. Clocks have never taken root in their culture. . . .

Some tribes measure a man's wealth, not by how much he accumulates, as white men do, but by how much in horses or silver or beadwork or blankets he gives away.

These last are not values around which modern industrial society is built. When Indians move into that society, it is not hard to see that the cultural conflict may spell disaster.

All sorts of curious and poignant, sometimes tragic, things may happen when the Indian is misunderstood just because there is something he, in turn, does not understand. There is a story of a boy in an off-reservation boarding school who, the neighboring farmer says, is stealing apples from his orchard. There is no doubt about the act; the farmer catches the boy red-handed. Yet the boy persists in declaring he is not stealing. . . . It all comes clear at last. On Jimmie's reservation there are no fences, no gates, and piñon nuts belong to anybody who wants to gather them. Jimmie has been away from his reservation home just long enough to know that things on the other side of the fence belong to somebody else but not long enough to know that you can't always tell about things when there isn't any fence. . . .

Everybody has familiar customs. Everybody has some values that are important to him. They influence the way he responds to life. They are the factors that make up this thing we call culture. And culture does make a difference.

There is something else besides culture that makes a difference in the life of many an Indian, and that is the stark fact of his poverty. . . .

Of the 400,000 persons counted as Indians in the United States today three-quarters have an income of $1,500 or below; the median figure is $725, as compared with a median of $2,619 for all American families. When you have to pay for rent and groceries and clothes for a whole family, a sum like this soon runs out.

For a key to social and economic adjustment in our society, we commonly look to education. . . . The median number of school years completed [by Indians] is fewer than eight. Somewhere between 15 and 20 per cent have never been to school at all. Of Indian children now of school age, almost 17 per cent are not enrolled in any school. . . .

With regard to responsibility, these are three chief points to keep in mind. First, the Indian himself is not at fault; he is the victim of such circumstances as historical isolation and cultural conflict. Second, direct relief is no real and lasting answer. We need to strike at the roots, at the causes of the poverty and the troubles that grow out of it. And third, no single group should

bear the blame or be faced alone with finding the solution. Government, church groups and other private
organizations, interested individuals, and Indians themselves can all help. If they work together, there can be
positive results. . . .

About three quarters of all Indians live on or near
their reservations or land that they once owned as reservations, land granted to them by treaty with the United
States Government. The larger share of their land is
unproductive, too barren of natural resources to support
its population. No Indian has to stay on the reservation, and many are leaving, some for work in agriculture, some for jobs in industrial centers. But migration
creates problems of its own.

And the Indian population is increasing! This sur-
prises many people who think of Indians as a dying
race. . . .

More and more Indians are joining the agricultural
migrant stream. The farm Placement Service found
jobs for 15,000 during 1953, and unknown numbers
went on their own, without going through the Government employment service. . . . Seeing them, you sense
the desperation that has driven them to long hours of
backbreaking work at substandard wages, far from their
home base and generally scorned by the very communities that recruit them.

Because it is the largest in area and population and
at the same time the most isolated, the Navaho country
shows most keenly the contrast between the life of many
Indians and that of the average white family. . . .

The life Ben [Chee Yazzie] leads with his mother
and father and three sisters and two brothers has scarcely
changed at all from the life his great-great-grandfather
led when 24,000 square miles of his homeland were set
aside as the Navaho Reservation back in 1868. On the

map it covers the northeastern corner of Arizona, the
northwestern corner of New Mexico, and a small slice
of southern Utah.

The Yazzie family make their home in a one-room
hogan with a dirt floor, no windows, and a smoke hole
in the roof. They herd sheep, sleep on goatskins, haul
water five miles for their spindling crop of corn and
squashes and melons, and when sickness strikes, they
call in the medicine man. More often than not his efforts
are ineffective and the patient dies, as Ben's small sister
did a year ago.

They spin the sheep's wool into yarn, color it with
bright clear vegetable dyes, and weave it into rugs and
blankets of traditional designs. They fashion silver and
turquoise into necklaces and bracelets and belts. Every
so often they climb into their ancient wagon, and the
family horse draws them eighteen miles to a trading
post, where they exchange what they have made for flour
and meal and dried fruit and coffee. Ben's mother and
sisters still wear the long flowing skirts and bright waists
copied by the Navaho women from the wives of General
Kit Carson's cavalry officers back in 1868.

There are two marked differences, though, between
then and now. For one thing erosion and overgrazing
have spoiled the land; the crop harvest has grown sparse,
and people and sheep are hungry. And for another
there are more people than ever before grubbing out a
living from the depleted land. For in spite of the fact
that the Navaho infant mortality rate is seven times the
national average and that the tuberculosis death rate is
nine times and the death rate from measles twenty-nine
times that of our general population—in spite of all this
—the 6,500 Navahos who took up life on the Reservation
under the Treaty of 1868 have become 70,000, and the
increase continues at the rate of a net 2.5 per cent each

year. Experts estimate that if the natural resources of the reservation were developed to fullest capacity, the land could support not more than 35,000, that is, about half of those now living there.

On other reservations the contrast with white communities is less marked, but all reservation life still lacks many of the conveniences most people regard as necessities for a comfortable existence. . . .

Indians are American citizens.

In every state in the nation, on and off reservations, Indians have the right to vote.

Indians need no permits to leave reservations nor to return to them.

Those three observations often seem to be news to many an American with a heart full of good will for Indians, a guilty conscience about America's treatment of them, and a head full of inaccuracies.

The fact is that an act of Congress in 1924 made citizens of all Indians. Many had previously been granted citizenship by law or treaty. . . .

On the reservation Indians are free to come and go when they choose, free to live and work where they choose, free to vote as they choose.

Just as they enjoy the privileges of citizenship, so are Indians subject to its obligations. Young Indian men are drafted into the army. Indian people pay taxes; personal income taxes, sales taxes, property taxes. The only exception to this is . . . [the] reservation land, which according to Government treaty remains tax-exempt.

What then do we mean by a special relationship between Indians and the Federal Government?

With tribe after tribe, it happened something like this: Settlers [Indians] began moving into smaller and smaller areas. In time one area would be defined by treaty as a reservation. In the treaty the Government promised to provide certain services for Indians remaining on the reservation. From the Indian viewpoint these services were accepted as a measure of compensation for lost land and a lost way of life.

What are these services? They fall into the broad categories of health, education, welfare and law enforcement, the kind of service the rest of the population receives from state or local agencies or private organizations. For the general population some of these services like public schools are free, some like hospital care are paid for on an individual basis.

When it originated, this policy of Federal protection and control seemed right and necessary. Today passing judgment on it is by no means simple. It has, however, had two results that have become a kind of undesirable psychological heritage of many Indians today.

One result has been to separate many Indians from the rest of the population, not only physically, but socially and spiritually. It has created a pattern of discrimination. It has made Indians feel different.

The other result has been to foster a feeling of dependence among Indians. The plan has failed to nourish initiative or to provide much incentive for Indians to help themselves.

Through the years much dedicated service and millions of dollars have been expended on behalf of Indians. Nevertheless, the problem has always been complex and thorny, super-charged with emotion on both sides. No one denies that there has been some lack of governmental understanding of Indian culture patterns. There has been too little opportunity for Indian people to share in working out plans for improving their own communities. There has been a degree of exploitation of Indians, both public and private; there has been some unwise administration with abrupt policy changes that made no sense at all to the Indians in whose interest they were sincerely supposed to operate.

Today if citizenship and franchise and freedom of movement make up the yardstick for measuring first-class citizenship, then Indians are first-class citizens. Yet many of them suffer through no fault of their own because they are confused about what to expect of the Government and what the Government expects of them. Democracy is a two-way street!

It takes education, education for all ages in the broadest sense, to overcome the effects of generations of paternalism—the lack of initiative, the feeling of inferiority, even of persecution that many Indians suffer. In this kind of education, the government, the missionaries, and the public can all help.

Four current trends in Indian government affairs call for intelligent scrutiny by every thoughtful citizen.

First there are the Government's efforts to help Indians develop economic resources on their reservations to raise their level of living. The Government provides credit for agricultural and commercial enterprises. It gives guidance in management of homes and farms, of forest and range, and it promotes soil and water conservation, develops irrigation projects and constructs and maintains roads.

These are intelligent programs, generally intelligently administered. The only catch is that they take money, and there never is enough. In an economy-minded Congress, all too often the Indian budget gets more than its share of cuts.

The second development is the Indian Bureau's relocation and placement program. [See Section V of this book.—Ed.] . . .

It lets Indians know about available opportunities for employment and assists those who want to take advantage of them. It is a small-scale experiment, and many Indians are migrating to cities without benefit of it. . . .

In addition to help for those who stay on the reservations and for those who leave, a third trend within the Indian Service is a strenuous effort to see that Indian children have an opportunity to go to school. Where there are public schools nearby, reservation children usually attend them. Federal aid goes to the school district for each Indian child attending. Otherwise, there are reservation day schools and boarding schools both on and off the reservation. Here again the great difficulty is there aren't enough! . . .

The fourth trend that we need to note is the gradual Federal withdrawal from Indian affairs.

As the Federal Government steps out, it is crucial that the Indian people understand what is happening and how they will be affected by it and that they accept the new way. Tribes need to be consulted, and their viewpoint reflected in the legislation that concerns them. This may be a long, slow process, but those who advocate it believe that Indians will benefit from legislative changes only if they themselves understand and accept new policies and procedures that affect their daily lives. . . .

Alice John Bedoni, nineteen, born and reared in the Toadalena Tohatchi section of the Navaho Reservation, gave the address as the representative of the Navaho graduating class [at the Government Indian school in Phoenix, Arizona], the group who five short years before had left their homes and come to the school to learn a new language and a new way of life. With no notes and no prompting, Alice stood erect with confident bearing and addressed the audience in English on her chosen theme: "Don't Let My People Down." . . .

Alice was speaking to her classmates and their families. Suppose instead she were talking, not to her commencement audience, but to a group of non-Indian friends. What would she say to them? What guidance might she give to them in a plea not to let her people down? The words she would choose we cannot tell, but might the ideas which she would present be something like these?

Look back into the story of our American nation, and see how much of our heritage has its roots in Indian culture. Look, and understand our pride in being Indian.

Study the ways of our tribes, and try to understand why it is not always easy for some of us to fit our ways to yours.

We want to be friends with you, to be at home in your world. Many of us want to make our contribution to your industry, to your church and community life, for we understand that your world has to be our world, too. But as we adapt our ways to yours, we do not want to forget that we are Indian.

Some of us are sensitive, and some of us are shy. Sometimes our names seem ludicrous to you. To us they have meaning and beauty, and we do not like you to laugh about them.

And please remember that we are just as different from one another as you and your brothers and sisters and friends are different from one another. Because some of us behave badly sometimes, do not decide that all of us are like that. Do not make of us that thing you call a stereotype.

Let the lawmakers in our Congress know that as they pass new laws affecting our people and our land we want to understand these laws and

what they mean for us. We want to share in the
planning of them.

What we want is opportunity. We will do the
rest. Do not let our people down.

POPULAR MISCONCEPTIONS [2]

Ever since the white men first fell upon them, the
Indians of what is now the United States have been
hidden from white men's view by a number of conflict-
ing myths. The oldest of these is the myth of the Noble
Red Man or the Child of Nature, who is credited either
with a habit of flowery oratory or implacable dullness
or else with an imbecile inability to converse in anything
more than grunts and monosyllables.

The first myth was inconvenient. White men soon
found their purposes better served by the myth of ruth-
less, faithless savages and later, when the "savages" had
been broken, of drunken, lazy good-for-nothings. All
three myths coexist today, sometimes curiously blended
in a schizophrenic confusion such as one often sees in
the moving pictures. Through the centuries the mythical
figure has been variously equipped; today he wears a
feather headdress, is clothed in beaded buckskin, dwells
in a tepee, and all but lives on horseback.

It was in the earliest period of the Noble Red Man
concept that the Indians probably exerted their most
important influence upon Western civilization. . . . The
French and English of the early seventeenth century
encountered, along the east coast of North America from
Virginia southward, fairly advanced tribes whose semi-
hereditary rulers depended upon the acquiescence of
their people for the continuance of their rule. . . . They

[2] From "Myths That Hide the American Indian," article by Oliver La
Farge, president, Association on American Indian Affairs, anthropologist, and
Pulitzer prize-winning author. *American Heritage, the Magazine of History.*
7:5-9+. October 1956. Reprinted by permission.

[the explorers] found that even the commonest subjects were endowed with many rights and freedoms, that the nobility was fluid, and that the commoners existed in a state of remarkable equality. . . .

A somewhat romanticized observation of Indian society and government, coupled with the idea of the Child of Nature, led to the formulation, especially by French philosophers, of the theories of inherent rights in all men, and of the people as the source of the sovereign authority. The latter was stated in the phrase, "consent of the governed." Both were carried over by Jefferson into our Declaration of Independence in the statement that "all men are created equal, that they are endowed by their Creator with certain inalienable Rights" and that governments derive "their just powers from the consent of the governed."

Thus, early observations of the rather simple, democratic organization of the more advanced coastal tribes, filtered through and enlarged by the minds of European philosophers whose thinking was ripe for just such material, at least influenced the formulation of a doctrine, or pair of doctrines, that furnished the intellectual base for two great revolutions and profoundly affected the history of mankind. . . .

Five of the Iroquois tribes achieved something unique in North America, rare anywhere, when in the sixteenth century they formed the League of the Five Nations— Senecas, Onondagas, Mohawks, Cayugas and Oneidas— to which, later, the Tuscaroras were added. The league remained united and powerful until after the American Revolution, and exists in shadowy form to this day. It struck a neat balance between sovereignty retained by each tribe and sovereignty sacrificed to the league, and as so durable and effective a union was studied by the authors of our Constitution. . . .

Had it not been for the white men's insatiable greed and utter lawlessness, this remarkable nation would have ended with a unique demonstration of how, without being conquered, a "primitive" people could adapt itself to a new civilization on its own initiative. They would have become a very rare example of how aborigines could receive solid profit from the coming of the white men.

After the five Civilized Tribes [Seminoles, Creeks, Choctaws, Chickasaws, and Cherokees of the Southeast-Mississippi Valley] were driven to Oklahoma, they formed a union and once again set up their governments and their public schools. Of course we could not let them have what we had promised them; it turned out that we ourselves wanted that part of Oklahoma after all, so once again we tore up the treaties and destroyed their system. None the less, to this day they are a political power in the state, and when one of their principal chiefs speaks up, the congressmen do well to listen. . . .

The tribes of the Atlantic coast were quickly dislodged or wiped out. The more advanced groups farther inland held out all through colonial times and on into the 1830's, making fairly successful adjustments to the changed situation, retaining their sovereignty, and enriching their culture with wholesale taking over of European elements, including, in the South, the ownership of Negro slaves. Finally, as already noted, they were forcibly removed to Oklahoma, and in the end their sovereignty was destroyed. They remain numerous, and although some are extremely poor and backward, others, still holding to their tribal affiliations, have merged successfully into the general life of the state, holding positions as high as chief justice of the state supreme court. [See "The Indians Among Us," in this section, below.—Ed.] The Iroquois still hold out in New York and in Canada on remnants of their original reservations. Many of them have had remarkable success in adapting themselves to white American life while retaining considerable elements of their old culture. Adherents to the old religion are many, and the rituals continue vigorously.

The British invaders of the New World, and to a lesser degree the French, came to colonize. They came in thousands, to occupy the land. They were therefore in direct competition with the Indians and acted accordingly, despite their verbal adherence to the principles of justice and fair dealing. The Spanish came quite frankly to conquer, to Christianize, and to exploit, all by force of arms. They did not shilly-shally about Indian title to the land or Indian sovereignty; they simply took over, then granted the Indians titles deriving from the Spanish crown. They came in small numbers—only around three thousand settled in the Southwest—and the Indian labor force was essential to their aims. Therefore they did not dislodge or exterminate the Indians, and they had notable success in modifying Indian culture for survival within their regime and contribution to it.

In the Southwest the few Spaniards, cut off from the main body in Mexico by many miles of difficult, wild country, could not have survived alone against the wild tribes that shortly began to harry them. They needed the Pueblo Indians and the Pueblos needed them. The Christian Pueblos were made secure in their lands and in their local self-government. They approached social and political equality. . . .

The Spanish, then, did not set populations in motion. That was done chiefly from the east. The great Spanish contribution was loosing the horses. They did not intend to; in fact, they made every possible effort to prevent Indians from acquiring horses or learning to ride. But the animals multiplied and ran wild; they spread from California into Oregon; they spread into the wonderful grazing land of the high Plains, a country beautifully suited to horses.

From the east, the tribes were pressing against the tribes farther west. Everything was in unhappy motion, and the tribes nearest to the white men had firearms. So the Chippewas, carrying muskets, pushed westward into Minnesota, driving the reluctant Dakotas, the Sioux tribes, out of the wooded country into the Plains as the horses spread north. At first the Dakotas hunted and ate the strange animals, then they learned to ride them, and they were off.

A new culture, a horse-and-bison culture, sprang up overnight. The participants in it had a wonderful time. They feasted, they roved, they hunted, they played. Over a serious issue, such as the invasion of one tribe's territory by another, they could fight deadly battles, but otherwise even war was a game in which shooting an enemy was an act earning but little esteem, but touching one with one's bare hand or with a stick was the height of military achievement. . . .

The Navahos staged a different cultural spurt of their own, combining extensive farming with constant horseback plundering, which in turn enabled them to become herdsmen, and from the captured wool develop their remarkable weaving industry. The sheep, of course, which became important in their economy, also derived from the white men. Their prosperity and their arts were superimposed on a simple camp life. With this prosperity, they also developed elaborate rituals and an astoundingly rich, poetic mythology. . . .

When the Plains culture died, the myth of it spread and grew to become imbedded in our folklore. Not only the northwest coast Indians but many others as unlikely wear imitations of Plains Indian costume and put on "war dances," to satisfy the believers in the myth. As it exists today in the public mind, it still contains the mutually incongruous elements of the Noble Red Man and the Bloodthirsty Savage that first came into being three centuries and a half ago, before any white man had ever seen a war bonnet or a tepee, or any Indian had ridden a horse.

THE ROLE OF CULTURE [3]

It has been a matter of constant astonishment to the Europeans who have been coming to the Western Hemisphere since the close of the fifteenth century that New World inhabitants did not rush upon them with open arms, like lost children, and avail themselves of the knowledge, skills, and customs of what the European has always thought of as the older and more advanced culture. The very term "New World" is a European concept implying that life in the Americas had no depth of antiquity and, therefore, had acquired no importance in world history.

Those who insist that the Indians must change their way of life if they are to survive are really insisting that the change must be made at once. They ignore or minimize the fact that Indians have been changing their habits, their material culture, and their outlook since the coming of the first white man. Gunpowder and bullets were readily substituted for bow and arrow. Woolen blankets and clothing, in northern climates at least, replaced heavy buffalo robes and deerhide leggings and

[3] From "A U.S. Indian Speaks," by D'Arcy McNickle, member of the Flathead tribe of Montana, director of the American Indian Development Foundation, and former official of the United States Bureau of Indian Affairs. *Américas.* 6:8-11+. March 1954. Reprinted by permission.

shirts. The trader's canned goods found prompt acceptance. Strong drink needed no sales promotion.

If the Indian accepted some objects and customs from the white world, why did he not accept them all? After adopting the steel axe, why not go at once into the forest, build a log cabin, and clear a field for planting? A steel axe made these things possible for the European because he was accustomed to building houses of wood or stone and to clearing and planting fields. The Indian, with as much logic, used the steel axe as a more effective tool for carrying on the kind of life he knew. With it he could cut down and dress tepee poles with greater ease. He could obtain wood for his fire with less effort. But the axe by itself was not enough to overturn a whole system of existence. . . .

The lot of this country's Indians is often compared —to their disadvantage—to that of our Negroes and of immigrants coming from other lands. A great part of United States history is made up of the life stories of penniless and persecuted minority groups from Europe who, rising above all handicaps of language and racial barriers, won acceptance and made their contributions. Negroes, rising out of slavery, have attained individual eminence in the arts and professions.

When in extenuation it is explained that Indians, by and large, are not competitive (there are, of course, individual exceptions) and have not made a virtue of acquisitiveness, the response is apt to be an incredulous stare. The implication is that if they are not competitive and acquisitive, they had better become so. This brings us at once to what is probably the root of the problem: People refuse or cannot bring themselves to believe that culture, an acquired quality, rules our actions, makes up our minds for us, and generally determines the events of our lives from birth to the final rites of passage. Rarely does it occur to any of us that our attitudes toward people, toward the physical universe, and toward the supernatural are not a universal characteristic of human nature. If no two people of the same race or even of the same family react in the same way to a given situation, it is even less likely that two people of diverse cultures would have the same reaction to a common problem. When rain fails and crops perish, the white man is apt to look to physical methods for relief; he sends an airplane into the sky and sprinkles certain mineral salts on cloud formations. The Hopi Indian goes into the desert, collects a variety of snakes, conducts a four-day prayer ceremony, then returns the snakes to the desert, for they are the messengers who will inform the gods of the situation on earth and send the life-saving rain. A man of Western culture will say emphatically that the Hopi Indian is ignorant and superstitious, but so far no one has persuaded a Hopi Rain Priest that he is wasting his time.

It is quite easy to fall into the habit of thinking of any culture that differs from our own as a transitory matter, something picturesque or brutish (depending on what aspect of the culture is viewed and who does the viewing)—in any case, something that will disappear when touched by reason. Because we underestimate the role of culture in determining men's actions, we often conclude that if a people does not change when the opportunity is offered, the reason can only be unrealistic stubbornness. It is but a step to the next conclusion: that if a people will not change of its own volition, pressure from the outside is justified. Much of the law-making in the field of Indian affairs in the United States, unfortunately, has been rooted in the mistaken belief that a legislative body can supply motivation and volition where these are lacking.

When, during the term of Commissioner John Collier [1933-1945], a major effort was made to work with and through surviving Indian cultures, it was called an unrealistic attempt to keep the Indians back in the Stone Age, to make museum pieces out of Indian societies for the edification of the curious. Defending the Indians' right to believe as they chose, to speak their own language, and to exercise self-government was considered mere sentimentality.

Those wh ̇ ̇ ̇ ̇ ̇ ̇ acquainted with the writings of Francisco ᵈᵃ V ̇ ̇ ̇ia know that the concept of Indians as human beings, with human rights, goes back to the very beginnings of European contact with the inhabitants of the Western Hemisphere. After advising Emperor Charles V, in 1532, that the Indians were "the true owners of the New World," Vitoria laid down this further principle: "The Christians have the right to preach the gospel among the barbarians . . . [but] they cannot be warred into subjection, whether they accept it or not." The right to own land or to bargain it away, the right to accept or reject an alien faith, were principles that would be many times confirmed as Europeans poured into the New World and built their societies. . . .

In discussing the future of the Indian people in the hemisphere, or more narrowly, in the United States, it is desirable always to know whether we are talking in terms of a short or a long view. It must be accepted as inevitable that Indian societies will disappear, that they have been in the process of dissolution and ultimate loss of identity from the beginning of white settlement. [But see "Outlook for the Indians," Section II, below.—Ed.] The question is: When will it happen and what will be the effect on the Indian people? Once we accept the inevitability of this change, it does not follow that dispersal of the Indians and destruction of their institutions is a desirable policy. The world has just lived through a period of madness in which a serious effort to obliterate a people was attempted. The effort failed, and the world may have been frightened into a measure of tolerance toward racial and cultural differences.

As a result either of population decline or of the amalgamation of two or more tribes under a single name, it is a fact that a number of tribes formerly occupying the area now known as the United States have disappeared. But more remarkable is the fact that Indians and Indian tribes have survived epidemics, removals, and the good intentions of a guardian protector. . . .

Survival is marked in more than numbers, tribal affiliations, languages, and property. Personality survives also, and the institutions that help to mold it. Even among those groups where religious and secular customs seem largely to have disappeared, traits of the old culture still persist. In a certain tribe where language and a brown skin seemed to be the only evidence of an Indian past, a young man in recent years became so successful at farming, using modern machinery and farming methods, that he earned $10,000 in a single year. Instead of being congratulated, the man was frowned upon by his relatives and neighbors. In the thinking of the past, only a stingy man or one helped by witches would accumulate so much wealth. The successful youngster had the choice of deserting his people (a difficult step for most Indians) or of curbing his ambitions in order to hold the respect of those closest to him. . . .

Now the question is raised: Should the policy with respect to the Indians of the United States continue in the direction laid down by the law of 1934 [Indian Reorganization Act, discussed in Section II, below]—the direction of orderly development and eventual transfer to the Indian people of responsibility and authority for the management of their own property and transfer, at the earliest possible date, of responsibility for services to state and local governments? . . .

Many people, including many Indians, feel that the adjustment can be made. Individually and by tribes, Indians have demonstrated that when properly motivated they can compete in a white man's world. The failure to bring about this adaptation up to now goes deeper than the deficiencies of any individual or any Government bureau. It has been a failure to understand the role of culture, a failure to see that culture shapes many of our ends, however much we try to hew them out by the force of reason.

Adjustment has to start with the people where they are, with their institutions, their outlook, the values they place on the events of life. You have to start from these and build in the desired direction. Simple as it may seem, this rule of procedure has rarely been followed in administering Indian affairs. The result has been . . . impatience, bewilderment, and frustration.

THE INDIANS AMONG US [4]

At colorful ceremonies in front of Oklahoma's capitol last January, N. B. Johnson, a Cherokee Indian, raised his hand and took the oath as chief justice of the Supreme Court of his state. Johnson had risen to Oklahoma's highest judicial office from a poor home on an Indian reservation. As president of the National Congress of American Indians for nine years, and president of the Inter-Tribal Council of the Five Civilized Tribes, Justice Johnson understands the unhappy lot of many American Indians. Not long ago he told me:

[4] From "Give the Indians an Even Chance," article by O. K. Armstrong, free-lance writer. *Reader's Digest*. 67:101-5. November 1955. Reprinted by permission.

"Let us help the surviving American Indian find his true place in our community and right the old wrongs. He can go to the top in every trade and calling if given equal opportunity with non-Indian citizens." . . .

The reservation Indian is born into a condition of inferiority. He grows up as a "ward of the Government." While Indians are free to move away from the reservations, the fear of racial discrimination and a feeling of incompetence prevent many from seeking a better life. . . .

Where barriers have been removed, Indians have become worthy members of their communities, and from them have come outstanding leaders. The Five Civilized Tribes of Oklahoma offer a striking example.

Years ago areas among their lands in the Indian Territory were opened for settlement by whites, and this intermingling weakened segregation. Ownership of the land by Indians was encouraged and Indian children went to public schools.

When Oklahoma became a state in 1907, Ben Harrison (Choctaw) and other Indian leaders helped to write the state constitution. Tribal governments were given up in exchange for full citizenship. Today Oklahoma Indians live with their neighbors on a basis of mutually helpful equality. The late humorist Will Rogers, who had Cherokee blood in his veins, was a product of this integration. Like the late Congressman William Stigler (Choctaw) and former Governor Johnston Murray (Chickasaw), Oklahoma Indians have held high public office.

Numbers of Indians from other states have filled and are filling positions of public trust in America. Charles Curtis of Kansas, proud of his Kaw Indian parentage, served as United States senator from Kansas for a quarter of a century and was Vice President of the

United States under Herbert Hoover. Ramon Roubi-
deaux (Sioux) was assistant attorney general of South
Dakota.

Many Indians are devoting their lives to helping their
own people. The career of Peru Farver (Choctaw) is
typical. He pushed on from Armstrong Academy to
study at Haskell Institute and Oklahoma A. & M. and
became superintendent of various reservations. Now he
is Tribal Relations Officer in the Public Health Service's
Division of Indian Health.

About half the Indian Bureau's personnel are of
Indian descent, as are half of its field employees. Most
of these left reservations for their advance schooling
and returned to serve their people. Fred H. Massey
(Choctaw) is chief of the Bureau's budget and finance.
Erma O. Hicks (Cherokee) is chief of Tribal Affairs.
Frank Hutchinson (Osage) is a key member of the
Bureau's Branch of Realty, and Carl Cornelius (Oneida)
is an officer on the Bureau's program-coordination staff.

Hervey Andrews, who retired last year after thirty
nine years of service with the Bureau, told me:

Reach out and take one handful of Indian children
and another handful of white children of comparable age
in any community, give them the same environment with
the same opportunities, and the white kids would have
trouble keeping up with their Indian companions.

Under the direction of the Bureau's education specialist, L. Madison Coombs, and Drs. Kenneth E. An-
derson and E. Gordon Collister of the University of
Kansas, fourteen thousand young Indians in seven states
were given achievement tests. Identical tests were given
to ten thousand non-Indian pupils in nearby communities.

The results of the tests indicate that from the fourth
grade to early teens Indian children prove about equal to

non-Indians. But at about fourteen the curve of ability starts lagging for Indian school children. The graphs for all the areas tested are too similar to be coincidental.

Mr. Coombs explains:

If, as the Indian child approaches maturity, he feels that his position in the social and economic world around him is not favorable, he may lose interest in his school-work. Specifically, he needs to feel that he will be socially accepted by the non-Indian community and have equal employment opportunity. Otherwise, education loses significance for him. This is possibly a partial explanation, at least, for the lag of achievement of Indian children at the higher grade levels.

Yet many Indians break through that barrier to become outstanding in their professions. Dr. Evelyn Yellow Robe went from her Rosebud Sioux Reservation to win degrees from Mt. Holyoke College and Northwestern University. Formerly a member of the faculty of Vassar College, she was recently awarded a Fulbright Scholarship for study in France. Roe B. Lewis (Pima), an authority on rural sociology, teaches in Cook Christian Training School at Phoenix, Arizona; Arthur C. Parker (Seneca) became one of America's foremost scholars in archeological research and Indian studies. Dr. George J. Frazier (Dakota) practiced medicine for forty-five years in the rural areas of South Dakota, inspiring many Indian youths to follow suit. Todd Downing (Choctaw) has written a number of mystery novels. Judge Erl Welsh (Chickasaw), former chief justice of Oklahoma's Supreme Court, is a leading member of the bar.

The myth of inferiority breaks down quickly when Indians are given opportunities to master skilled trades. Victor Manuel (Pima) worked in the print shop of his school and learned English as he set type. In 1923 he was one of the organizers of Arizona Printers, Inc., which grew to be a thriving enterprise. During the last two decades men of the Six Nations tribes have become noted for their ability as structural-steel workers. Indians of many western tribes are proving adept in the expanding field of electronics.

A supervising nurse in a Los Angeles hospital told me: "Because of their skill with instruments, plus their natural patience, Indian girls make the best nurses in the world."

There are noted Indian names in music and art. Maria Tallchief (Osage) is one of the world's leading ballerinas. Mobley Lushanya (Chickasaw), dramatic soprano, made her debut with the Chicago City Opera and has since achieved stardom in grand opera, concerts and radio, appearing as soloist with the London Philharmonic and other orchestras. Dr. Jack Kilpatrick (Cherokee), professor of music at Southern Methodist University, has composed more than 155 works, including symphonies, concertos and musical dramas. He wrote the music for the highly successful play *Unto These Hills,* presented each summer on the reservation at Cherokee, N.C.

Richard West (Cheyenne), who is an art instructor at Bacone College and whose paintings hang in numerous galleries, conducted me through the rooms, displaying the works of his students. "All Indian youths display an artistic trend," he declared.

The late Jim Thorpe (Sac-Fox) is recognized as one of the greatest athletes who ever lived. In 1912 he won both the pentathlon and decathlon at the Olympic games. "Chief" Charles Bender (Chippewa) began his baseball career in 1903 as pitcher with the Philadelphia Athletics, hung up a record of 212 games won, 128 lost, and is classed by sports authorities as one of the top pitchers of all time. Following such examples, Indian youths today excel in all forms of athletics.

Guy Jennison, chief of the Ottawas and a former county commissioner, is typical of Indians who have made a good living from the soil. As I walked with him over his fertile acres outside Miami, Okla., he said: "My son and I take pride in this farm because we own it. Let all Indians own their land, and you'll find them taking their places among the best farmers and ranchers in America." Another such farmer is John Long (Ute) who in 1953 won a distinguished-farmer award for his accomplishment in taking an old farm, cleaning it up, planting the soil to improved alfalfa and other productive crops and constructing a new home for his family.

Indian warriors have served ably with our armed forces in both world wars and in Korea. Many have made the military a career.

At the Intermountain Indian School in Utah, where 2,500 teen-age Navaho youngsters study, I watched the bronzed, hearty boys and girls filing from dormitories to classes, to workshops and to dining halls. All had come from an impoverished, highly segregated reservation. In a few years, after more schooling, all would be ready for good jobs and homemaking. Thoughtfully Dr. George A. Boyce, the superintendent, remarked:

"There go the Indian leaders of the next generation —one of America's greatest assets!"

INDIAN GIFTS TO OUR CULTURE [5]

The changes that American Indians wrought in the life of our pioneers were far more impressive and less destructive than any changes "white" teachers have yet

[5] From "American Indians: People Without a Future," by Ralph Nader, president, *Harvard Law Record*. *Harvard Law Record*. 22:2-6. April 5, 1956. Reprinted by permission.

brought to Indian life. Early settlers recognized that
Indian modes and methods were functionally adapted to
their physical environment. Four-sevenths of our national farm produce consists of plants domesticated by Indian botanists of pre-Columbian times. Indian agricultural products also had a tremendous impact on the
European economy. The story of the potato in Europe
need not be retold. Methods of planting, irrigation,
cultivation, storage and utilization were also acquired
by settlers from the Indians.

In medicine, as in the production of food and textiles,
the conventional picture of the Indian as an ignorant
savage is far removed from the truth. Cocaine, quinine,
cascara sagrada, ipecac, arnica and other drugs were
developed and used by the Indian before Columbus
landed. In the four hundred years that physicians and
botanists have been examining and analyzing the flora
of America, they have not yet discovered a medicinal
herb unknown to the Indians. The social significance
of such material contributions is impressive.

As is being illustrated in "underdeveloped" countries
today, a change in the material living standard inevit-
ably influences, destroys, and creates institutional patterns and modes of behavior. The impact of Indian
material culture undoubtedly has had important reper-
cussions on our society from our economy to the homestead system, and in land use, athletics, our boy scout
movement and our national worship of sun, air, and
water.

But the Indian gave more in the realm of the in-
tangible. The distinctive political ideals of young America owed much to a rich Indian democratic tradition—a
debt often recognized by statements of our leading colonists. The pattern of states within a state that we call
federalism, the habit of treating chiefs as servants of

the people instead of masters, the insistence that the community must respect the diversity of men and their dreams—all these things were part of the American way of life before 1492.

Franklin carried his admiration for the great Iroquois Confederacy to the Albany Congress, and Jefferson made numerous references to the freedom and democracy of Indian society which achieved the maximum degree of order with the minimum degree of coercion. The late Felix Cohen, noted legal scholar and Indian authority, remarked:

> Those accustomed to the histories of the conqueror will hardly be convinced, though example be piled on example, that American democracy, freedom and tolerance are more American than European, and have deep aboriginal roots in our land.

At this point the reader may well ask: "Of what relevance is this buried legacy to the present and future?" First, there is still much that the Indian can contribute to our cultural enrichment. Indian ingenuity in agriculture, government, medicine, sports, education and craftsmanship is not at an end.

Let a few examples do for many. Not long ago, the rediscovery of an old Indian dish, toasted corn flakes, revolutionized the breakfast routine of American families. A classic study of Cheyenne law by the anthropologist E. Adamson Hoebel and Professor Karl Llewellyn provided insights into our own jurisprudence. Indian methods of child training have caught the attention of psychiatrists and pediatricians, who are now comparing these methods with the rigid schedules and formulas that have molded our antiseptic babies of recent decades.

Second, recognition by legislators, administrators and the American public of the true nature of our Indian heritage has great importance in freeing the Indian from a contemptuous and grotesque stereotype. It also may diminish the persistent themes of pity, superiority and the white man's burden, which have been twisted into a vicious weapon against Indian culture and landholdings. Respect for different cultures may bring about a reasoned and humane policy which will fulfill Indian desires to achieve a higher living standard and still maintain his ethnic identity.

II. HISTORY OF INDIAN-WHITE
RELATIONS

EDITOR'S INTRODUCTION

Since the advent of the white man on this continent, the Indian has suffered at his hands. Sometimes it has been by attempts to "civilize" or "Christianize" the "savage," sometimes by the greed of land-grabbers with Government backing, sometimes by an excess of misguided paternalism. The most recent issue between the races concerns the determination of many of those charged with supervision of Indian affairs to liquidate the unsolved problems of 175 years and "get out of the Indian business."

This section opens with a review of Indian-Federal relations. The administration of John Collier as Commissioner of Indian Affairs under the Indian Reorganization Act of 1934, a turning point in our treatment of the Indians, is evaluated in the next article, which is followed by three critical surveys of recent changes in our Indian policy.

The present Commissioner next sets forth the aims of his administration. This is followed by a free-lance writer's vigorous indictment of the treatment of the Indian by our Government and our non-Indian population.

Closing this section is a summary of conclusions reached by a group of anthropologists discussing Indian problems. It dismisses some of the most common assumptions underlying public discussion of these problems and concludes that the Indians will resist all at-

tempts to swallow them up in a white man's civilization
and will continue to exist indefinitely as "cultural islands"
in the United States.

HISTORY OF PAST 175 YEARS [1]

To understand many of the problems Indians face
today, it is necessary to consider some of the basic
changes in the tribes' relationship to the Government of
the United States over the past 175 years.

In the beginning, the Federal Government regarded
the tribes as separate nations—a concept adopted by
the first colonists and elaborated upon by the Constitution and decisions of the courts.

When the Government warred against the tribes,
or attempted to force their removal from territories
coveted by miners or settlers, it dealt with them as bodies
having the power of self-government. Treaties made
with the chiefs and headmen of the various Indian
groups were considered binding on all members. The
Indians expected the agreements to be permanent obligations of the United States.

During this early period, the Federal Government
made little conscious effort to alter Indian culture. The
policy was clearly expressed by Henry Knox, first Secretary of War and Indian administrator, who said: "The
civilization of the Indians would be an operation of
complicated difficulty; it would require the highest
knowledge of human character, and a steady persever-
ance in a wise system over a series of years."

Busy pushing the harassed tribesmen ever westward
and forcing them from their vast hunting grounds on to
inadequate reservations, the American people had little

[1] From *The Spirit They Live In*, pamphlet. American Friends Service
Committee. 20 South 12th Street. Philadelphia 7. April 1956. p7-13. Reprinted by permission.

time for painstaking efforts. The "civilization" of the Indians was largely left to a relative handful of Protestant and Catholic missionaries.

Shortly after the Civil War, all but a few Indians had been settled on reservations, many far from their ancestral homelands. Greatly reduced in numbers by war, starvation and disease, most of the tribes were in danger of extinction. Some few were partially self-supporting, but most had to depend on the army which had conquered them for food and clothing.

It was at this point that Congress made the first of three major policy decisions which altered the historic concept of Indian-Government relations. In 1871, Congress declared that it would legislate for the tribes as for the rest of the population. This meant the end of treaty-making, and brought the internal affairs of the tribes into the purview of Congress. In the years that followed, not only tribal matters but family relations and even individual liberties were controlled by men who often had little knowledge of the needs and desires of the Indian people.

The second great policy decision was the General Allotment Act of 1887, which authorized the President to subdivide tribally owned lands into individual parcels, without consent of the Indian group affected. The avowed purpose of the act was to abolish what was an almost universal system of Indian land tenure, and one of the most cohesive forces in tribal life. Many responsible church leaders were among those who argued that private land holding would almost automatically "civilize" the Indians.

Congress was apparently trying to effect a quick legislative cure for what many felt were social ills. A better and more lasting remedy, perhaps, might have been a broad educative program; but few in authority were willing to undertake anything as difficult, time-consuming and initially expensive as the education of a people. Civilization by fiat was simpler, particularly when it meant only cutting up the Indians' own land, and selling what remained after allotment as "surplus."

Land allotment, contrary to the predictions of its well-intentioned supporters, did little to "civilize" any Indian group. On the contrary, it did much to impoverish many Indians and prevent their making their fullest contribution to society. In the four decades after 1887, some 88 million acres—or 63 per cent—of the tribes' richest agricultural, grazing, mining and timber land went into non-Indian hands.

During the same period, Indian population increased approximately 40 per cent, from 290,000 to 406,000. A greatly reduced land base and steadily increasing population left an estimated 100,000 Indians without resources; they were forced to make their homes as squatters on cutover forest lands, on vacant city lots and on town dumps.

Public reaction to reports of these tremendous land losses, and to the revelations contained in the Meriam Report of 1928, forced Congress to make the third major change in its Indian policy: the Indian Reorganization Act of 1934. Though admittedly incomplete, the act represented, in many respects, a return to long-forgotten principles of just and honorable treatment for Indians. . . .

While the blessings of the Indian Reorganization Act were not spread too evenly across Indian country, most tribes and many individual Indians did move toward self-sufficiency during this period.

But the era of good feeling ended abruptly in 1953 with passage of House Concurrent Resolution 108. This measure states in part:

It is the policy of Congress, as rapidly as possible, to make the Indians within the United States subject to the same laws and entitled to the same privileges and responsibilities as are applicable to other citizens of the United States, to end their status as wards of the United States, and to grant them all of the rights and prerogatives pertaining to American citizenship.

Passage of this resolution, and proposal of the "termination" bills which followed it, did much to confuse the already complex Indian situation and to divert attention from the real needs of Indians.

During the past three years, the energies of thousands of elected officials and government employees have been devoted to implementing the new Indian policy. The Senate and House have held scores of hearings, and new branches have been set up with the Bureau of Indian Affairs to plan and program the government's withdrawal from Indian administrative responsibility. In area offices and reservation agencies, staffs have been kept busy planning the transfer of various services, inventorying property, and appraising the competence of Indians to manage their own affairs.

Forced concentration on termination has given Indian Bureau personnel little time to find ways of helping Indians solve the basic problems which confront them. True, the Bureau has devoted increasing time and funds to its relocation program, the resettlement of reservation Indians in urban areas, but this program has won acceptance as a new technique for encouraging rapid "assimilation."

Tribal resistance to hasty termination, coupled with aroused public concern, resulted in the defeat of half the termination bills introduced for specific tribes in the Eighty-third Congress, and apparently gave pause to those who would have abruptly changed the Indian-Government relationship.

Still, it can be said that little is being accomplished today. Termination remains the official Federal policy, and opposition to premature change continues as the prime objective of most Indians and groups concerned with their welfare. In a sense, both positions are negative, for they prevent concentration on the essential task of finding ways to meet the needs of Indians, both as individuals and as members of communities. . . .

In states where Federal responsibilities and services to Indians have already been terminated or curtailed, state funds are being expended in increasing amounts on Indian education, health, welfare assistance, law enforcement and resource management. A number of states recently have created quasi-official commissions to deal with tribal matters.

Tribal governments are bearing an ever-greater share of the service burden. On some reservations, the entire income derived from tribal business enterprises is being spent on programs formerly financed and administered by the Federal Government.

The transfer of responsibility to the states, the tribes and even to counties and municipalities, has not resulted in substantial improvement in Indian living conditions, or made possible the development of reservation resources. On the contrary, it seems to have slowed the movement toward self-sufficiency which began with the Indian Reorganization Act. Apparently, there can be little hope of widespread progress until Indians are assured a greater measure of self-determination, and until the tribes and the government can feel free to seek common positive approaches to their problems.

INDIAN REORGANIZATION ACT [2]

The groundwork for a change [in the United States Government's Indian policies] was laid in 1928 when Lewis Meriam and his associates published their Institute of Government Research report, *The Problems of Indian Administration*. In this comprehensive and fundamental study, the failure of the assimilation policy was boldly drawn, and practical, specific recommendations were made. Under President Hoover, Charles Rhoads and J. H. Scattergood administered the Indian Office and began making the Government a helpful friend instead of a despotic manager. A good spirit of cooperation between the Government and the Indians came about. New emphasis on day schools marked the beginning of a better educational policy. Tribal skepticism and the novelty of the approach slowed the work, but a new day had definitely begun.

John Collier became Commissioner of Indian Affairs in 1933. For a number of years he had headed the militant Indian Defense Association, had saved the Pueblo lands from seizure by associates of Albert B. Fall by forcing the defeat of the anti-Indian Bureau bill, and had demonstrated his devotion to the Indian cause in many other ways.

Collier's plan was to make a clean sweep of the old ways and make it possible for Indians to live as Indians until a more natural and less destructive assimilation could come about, no matter how long that might take. His first step was to get through a none-too-willing Congress the Wheeler-Howard bill, largely his own work, assisted by Nathan Margold and Felix Cohen, Interior Department attorneys. In the end this emerged almost

[2] From "Whither the American Indian?" by Alden Stevens, free-lance writer. *Survey Graphic* 29:168-74. March 1940. Reprinted by permission.

intact as the Indian Reorganization Act, and it is the legal basis for Collier's program.

The act does not apply to any tribe which rejects it in an election, and though it does not appear that a tribe has anything to lose by accepting it, a considerable number have voted it down, including the Navahos. The Administration frankly urges its adoption, sometimes with a fairly high pressure campaign, but there is no evidence of discrimination against those who reject it and nothing to cast suspicion on any of the elections. . . .

The allotment policy [initiated in 1887] is ended and, while present holdings of individuals are not affected, no more allotments will be made. Indian owners of reservation land may now sell it, but only to the tribe, a provision which prevents further alienation of Indian land. Ceded lands which have neither been alloted nor settled by whites are returned to the tribe, and provision is made for small additions to Indian holdings where necessary. Management is by an elected tribal council, which (except where there is a shortage) assigns each member as much land as he can actually use. Thus one of the worst administrative headaches is on the way to a cure, and the shrinkage of Indian holdings is halted except for some of those tribes which have rejected the Reorganization Act. It is true that the problems of the checkerboarded reservations are not solved, and most of the old difficulties of rental and division of proceeds among heirs of allotees remain. But the new policy does turn land management back to the Indians; it goes far toward stabilization of the situation, and it seems to be working out well in most places.

No less important than the land provisions are the sections of the Reorganization Act enabling Indians to organize, adopt a constitution, and to incorporate. These give a measure of self-government greater than ever enjoyed before, though approval of the Secretary of the Interior is still required on many important matters. The constitutions are supposed to originate with the tribes, but Government lawyers have usually helped frame them, and each must be approved by the Secretary before the tribe votes acceptance or rejection.

It is the Secretary of the Interior, too, who issues a charter of incorporation when petitioned to do so. This also is subject to a vote on the reservation. Indians have never before had an opportunity to do much voting on what they wanted or didn't want, and not all tribes have taken kindly or intelligently to the democratic process thrust suddenly upon them under the New Deal. On some reservations, such as the Hopi, the idea of an all-tribal elected council is so foreign that many Indians simply do not recognize its authority and pay little attention to its activities. Poorly educated people commonly miss the full implications of an election and ignore it. After it is over they may resent the powers acquired by the council members and regard them simply as Government stooges.

Congress is authorized to appropriate $10 million as a revolving fund from which loans may be made to these chartered corporations for the purposes of promoting the economic development of the tribes. Repayments are credited to the revolving fund and are available for new loans. It was this fund which made possible the fresh start of the Mescalero Apache tribe. The record of collections on these loans has been very good.

About seventy-five of the tribal corporations are now functioning [in the sixth year of the Reorganization Act], with varying degrees of success, and the number continues to grow. The Jicarillas have bought their trading post and are running it; the Chippewas run a tourist camp; the Northern Cheyennes have a very successful livestock corporation; the Swinomish of Washington have a tribal fishing business. There are plenty of others to prove these corporations can be made to work.

So far, however, it has shown up best where a small, close-knit group is involved, but less satisfactorily on such large reservations as those of the Sioux, where distances are great and there is a certain amount of mutual distrust and jealousy between communities. Smaller cooperatives, at least for the present, may be indicated.

In the case of the Blackfeet, the tribal council, when elected, proved to be predominantly Indians of mixed blood, and the full bloods of the population complained that their interests were being subordinated and neglected wherever they conflicted with those of the mixed bloods. The election system was adjusted later to insure fair representation of the minority group. The difficulty about the system is that so many Indians on large reservations—and some on small—do not have a sense of common interest. The nine Hopi villages in Arizona have a long tradition of independent action as city states, with very little cooperation or friendly feeling between them. In other cases the desperately poor circumstances prevailing and the lack of resources to start with have caught tribes simply too run down and discouraged to put their shoulders to the wheel.

But all this new machinery gives Indians for the first time an opportunity to run their own affairs, to a limited extent, it is true, but previously everything was handled by the Government, and the Indians had to take it or leave it. Now a tribe, as a corporation, may purchase, operate and dispose of property, may hire counsel, engage in business enterprises of nearly any sort, and generally enjoy the legal privileges of a corporation. Management by the elected council is not always good, but at least it is management by Indians through democratic processes, and a period of adjustment to the new way must be expected to produce mistakes and failures as well as successes. It has all been thrust upon the tribes very suddenly as such things go—too suddenly, say critics of the Administration, and they may be right. . . .

No discussion of Collier's policies would be complete without mention of an important trend within the Office of Indian Affairs. The Reorganization Act is designed to set up mechanisms within the tribe which will perform the social services now provided by the Government bureau. The result should be a gradual withering of the bureau as the new tribal machinery takes over the load. . . . Complete elimination of the bureau cannot be "accomplished for many years, if ever, and meanwhile Indians are being trained and encouraged to seek government positions in it. . . . These men and women are getting valuable experience in public administration, and as the office decreases in size many of them will be prepared to step into tribal government and perform there the greatest possible service to their people. . . .

An improved system of administration of justice to Indians was deleted from the Wheeler-Howard bill before passage. However, the judicial power of the reservation superintendents, once almost unlimited, has been sharply reduced, and the Government has much less control over individual lives and activities than it formerly had. . . .

Many sober observers have charged that Collier's program has been jammed through much too fast, and that this speed has brought about more trouble and resentment than it was worth. The Indian Rights Association, which has worked tirelessly for Indians since 1882, points to the good work of the previous [Hoover]

Administration as proof that it is not necessary to go so fast, and that orderly progress following careful experiment may result in more permanent reform with less upsetting opposition. There is evidence that the pace has now slowed down. . . .

Nothing has stirred up so much antagonism in the Indian country as the driving passion for immediate and complete reform, the impatience with criticism and the too enthusiastic press notices which have been characteristic since Collier took over.

Other critics have called Collier visionary, and his policies communistic. Some say Indians do not want to and are not competent to govern themselves. Occasionally, on the other hand, we hear that Collier is a sentimentalist, trying to hold the Indian back for the benefit of tourists and anthropologists, to keep him out of the main stream of American life. These groups, however, apparently have nothing to suggest but a return to the old assimilation policy which gave no promise of success and every evidence of complete and tragic failure during the long years of its history. . . .

It has been a terrific problem. Hopelessly tangled in obsolete laws, nearly landless, poverty stricken, uneducated, prey to white interests everywhere, unable to defend themselves, and finally saddled with an administrative policy which regarded them as a dying people, more in need of race euthanasia than anything else, the Indians could hardly have been worse off. As far back as 1862 Abraham Lincoln said, "If we get through this war, and I live, this Indian system shall be reformed." But it is only now that this is really taking place.

The truth is that the New Deal Indian administration is neither as successful as its publicity says it is, nor as black and vicious a failure as the severest critics would have us believe. Many Indian problems remain unsolved, but every one has been attacked. If eddies have been stirred up, there is still a powerful current in Indian affairs, and it seems to be in a direction which gives this splendid race an opportunity to shape its own destiny.

VAGARIES OF U.S. POLICY [3]

In more than three centuries of association with this [Indian] race, we have tried nearly everything. Some of the early European invaders tried enslavement, and that failed. Others tried to divide and rule and that did not accomplish the desired results. From time to time there have been local attempts at extermination. These did not succeed, although they came closer than we like to think. Then many people, including some missionaries, tried to make the Indian over in our image, without conspicuous or lasting success. The policy followed by our Government with most persistence has been to isolate the Indian, first in underdeveloped parts of the country, and then on reservations. But that has not worked either.

Since the beginning of this century our Government has spent more than $1 billion to improve the economic condition of this minority. But the simple materialistic faith that filling stomachs solves all other problems, which seems to underlie our policy toward underdeveloped countries threatened with communism, has not solved the problem of our relations with the Indians. The only policy we have not tried consistently, determinedly and on a large scale is the policy of study of the Indian heritage, respect for the Indian as an individual and for his social groupings as essential to his way of life and persistent, long-term cooperation on the basis of full Indian understanding and consent toward the realization

[3] From "Indian Winter," article by Harold E. Fey, editor, *Christian Century*. *Christian Century* 72:265-7. March 2, 1955. Reprinted by permission. This material is to be incorporated in a forthcoming book, *Indians and Other Americans*, by Harold E. Fey.

of a good life for both races in the continental home we occupy together. . . .

When we set out to help the Indian overcome his . . . distrust, we encounter a hard fact of which we had been only dimly aware: the policy of the United States toward our 400,000 Indians has recently changed. Congress at least has said it has changed. Indians are not surprised at one more change after so many, but they consider the latest change one which is not in their favor. The organizations which are interested in Indian welfare agree with the Indian leaders holding this opinion. Charges are made that under the new policy the Federal Government will violate treaty obligations and other agreements and laws. The Indians are aware that most Americans know nothing about what is being done. They wonder if they would care if they knew. Their friends seem few and ineffectual.

An attempt to discover whether the Indians' feeling is justified leads us straight to House Concurrent Resolution 108, which was passed in 1953. It declares that Congress has decided to "make" Indians conform to the laws which bind everybody else and "to end their status as wards of the United States." This is to be done "as rapidly as possible." When this process is completed the Indians will have the privileges, rights and responsibilities of all other citizens. The resolution says the Indians "should assume their full responsibilities as American citizens." Isn't that good?

Ask the Indian. He says it means he will have to pay taxes on his land, and that this is unjust. Why shouldn't he pay taxes on his land? He says its tax-free status was bought by him when he made concessions of larger territories on condition that this land was to be his without conditions. He asks what the holders of tax-free municipal bonds would say if the government were suddenly to make them "assume their full responsibilities as citizens" by paying taxes on these bonds.

He inquires what manufacturers who have built plants useful for national defense after being promised tax concessions would say if suddenly Congress were to decide they had to pay taxes on these buildings. He points out that educational institutions, cooperatives and churches are not taxed; that owners of oil wells do not have to pay taxes on 27 per cent of their output as a depletion allowance. All these concessions were made for reason, the Government receiving full value for the concession. The Government has also received full value from the Indians, as expressed in nearly four hundred treaties. But H.R. 108 means that Congress declares it is the policy of the United States to renounce its end of these bargains without returning to the Indians the valuable considerations they gave for this exemption.

The bills deriving from H.R. 108 do more than withdraw Federal trust from Indian properties placed on tax rolls. They also terminate the application of the Indian Reorganization Act of 1934, abolish tribal constitutions and corporations based on that law, abrogate Federal-Indian treaties, and impose the breakup of tribal properties into individual parcels. But the basis of the Indian's apprehension is that these bills threaten his land. He remembers what happened as a result of the Indian Allotment act of 1887: Indian landholdings shrank from 139 million to 48 million acres.

What considerations caused Congress to adopt H.R. 108? It is not easy to discover because no hearings were held on the highly important policy statement contained in this resolution before it was adopted. When I inquired in the Indian Bureau in Washington as to its meaning, I was told that it was not accurate to say the Government had adopted a "termination program." Commissioner

Glenn Emmons, I was told, does not like the words "termination" or "withdrawal." I was informed that the expressed intent of Congress has no force until individual laws are passed making the intent apply to a particular tribe. H.R. 108 names thirteen tribes, but Congress terminated only six, so the policy applies to six. The Indian Bureau official assured me that the bureau knows H.R. 108 has created a "state of psychological shock" among Indians across the country; that it hopes Congress will not enact more such laws until it sees what happens in the cases of the six. I was not able to learn who wrote 108, except that I was told it was not written in the Indian Bureau. . . .

While no hearings were held on the question of policy as to whether the Federal Government should end Indian wardship, hearings were held on termination as it affected the groups or tribes mentioned in the operative part of the resolution. These took testimony on whether the particular tribes were ready to manage their own affairs, to pay taxes on their land in addition to other taxes which they pay already, their educational and economic status, and so forth. In addition hearings were held on an earlier resolution, H.R. 89, which was enacted March 25, 1953. This resolution asked the Indian Bureau to supply a list of tribes ready for "full management of their own affairs," and for "legislative proposals designed to promote the earliest practicable termination of all Federal supervision and control over Indians.". . .

But the Indian Bureau also contributed in a series of actions beginning in 1950 and ending in the collection of data concerning preparedness for termination of each tribe or group in the United States. The commissioner of Indian affairs in the period of 1950-53 was Dillon S. Myer, who had previously headed the governmental organization which supervised the relocation of Japanese-

Americans. His administration of the Indian Bureau was the subject of a devastating analysis by Felix S. Cohen in the *Yale Law Review* for February 1953. Mr. Cohen, now deceased, was a leading authority on laws which apply especially to Indians, having compiled the four thousand statutes which had been enacted before 1940 when he was on the staff of the Department of the Interior. He pointed out that beginning in May 1950, when Mr. Myer took office, Indian freedom began to be restricted, Indian property was increasingly controlled by the bureau, and that arm of the Government was transformed into an instrument of power.

So the "erosion of Indian rights" which is observable today started several years ago in a Democratic Administration. A similarly gradual turn occurred over twenty-five years ago when the last previous important change in national policy toward the Indians took place.

That was a change toward more freedom. It began in the Coolidge Administration in 1924 when the Indians were given the right to vote and in 1926 when Secretary of the Interior Hubert Work asked the Brookings Institution to survey the economic and social conditions of the Indians. This survey resulted in the famous Meriam report, issued in 1928, from which later progress got its start. It continued in the Hoover Administration with the appointment of two Quakers as commissioner and assistant commissioner of Indian affairs. Charles J. Rhoads, Philadelphia banker, and J. Henry Scattergood, treasurer of Haverford and Bryn Mawr colleges, have chiefly to their credit the revival and modernization of Indian education. They got Congress to increase its appropriations for education from $3 to $12 million a year.

From this background came the Indian Reorganization Act of 1934, which opened the way to two decades of Indian progress. Congress gave the Indians the right to establish corporations, and two thirds of the tribes took advantage of the opportunity. (Some of the recent termination bills abolished these corporations but gave the Indians the right to set up others.) Indian tribal councils were given greater authority. They could veto disposal of Indian property by the Indian Bureau and had access to a $10 million credit fund for developing tribal resources. Indians got preference for Indian Bureau jobs. But the Indian Reorganization act was only a beginning.

In 1935 Congress set up an agency to market Indian handicrafts. Indians began to use the right to vote, and the last states to withhold the right—New Mexico and Arizona—yielded it in 1948. In 1938 the Supreme Court recognized that minerals and timber on Indian reservations belong to the Indian and not to the Government. In 1940 Congress refunded the taxes Indians had been forced to pay when thousands of tax-exempt estates were terminated without Indian consent. (What will the courts say concerning the present termination laws if Indians declare they were enacted without their consent, causing them to lose their land and resources?) In 1941 the Supreme Court upheld the right of Indians to lands they had long occupied, even without formal treaties or acts of Congress. During the war thousands of young Indians served in the armed forces. In 1946 an Indian Claims Commission was set up by Congress to help Indians collect the debts they said the Government owed them. In 1948 the Supreme Court helped the Indian as well as other minority races when it ruled that racially restrictive covenants are "unenforceable." By 1949 no state claimed the right to discriminate against the Indian in old age assistance, aid to the blind, aid to dependent children. Two years later the Indian got access to farm housing loans.

Note what these actions accomplished. An atmosphere of hope and optimism spread over the Indian reservations. For the first time in eighty years Indian holdings of land increased—from 48 to 52 million acres. Real Indian income doubled. The death rate was cut in half. The condition of the Indian generally improved.

With 1950 the atmosphere began to change. "Like the miner's canary, the Indian marks the shifts from fresh air to poison gas in our political atmosphere," said Mr. Cohen, "and our treatment of Indians, even more than our treatment of other minorities, reflects the rise and fall of our democratic faith." The Indians were the first to suffer from the shock to our democratic institutions produced by fear of communism and the outbreak of the Korean war. In the Indian Bureau this coincided with the beginning of the Myer regime, which took over just before the outbreak of war in Korea brought a general restriction of freedom and a preoccupation with events abroad. So nobody paid much attention when elections of tribal officers were interfered with on the Blackfeet reservation in Montana. Land belonging to the San Ildefonso pueblo in New Mexico was sold without Indian consent. The right of certain tribes to select their own legal counsel was challenged for the first time in years, and the American Bar Association appointed a commission which rebuked the Indian Bureau for going beyond its authority. . . .

The practice of consulting Indians on legislation or other matters affecting their welfare was virtually stopped. Some tribes found it impossible to obtain statements concerning balances in their tribal funds on deposit with the United States Treasury. They got a unanimous ruling from the Indian Claims Commission that withholding of such information from properly authorized persons was illegal.

There is good reason to believe and to hope that the present commissioner, Glenn L. Emmons, formerly a Gallup, New Mexico, banker, has done much to change for the better the temper and procedures of the Indian Bureau administration. My own experience with bureau personnel in several states made me believe that all of the officials I met were honestly working for Indian welfare to the limit of their very considerable abilities. They are however limited by the policies laid down by Congress. They are also fenced in by the Department of the Interior, in which the Indian Bureau is domiciled. The policies of that department concerning public lands and other resources impinge upon Indian life at many points. Officials who desire to place humanitarian considerations first are keenly aware that the Secretary of the Interior may be more concerned for the uninhibited operation of private enterprise than he is for Indian welfare.

A CRITICAL REVIEW OF THE RECORD [4]

One of the earliest statements on [Federal] policy [on Indian affairs] is found in Article 3 of the Northwest Ordinance of Congress, dated July 13, 1787. It reads: "The utmost good faith shall always be observed towards the Indians; their lands and property shall never be taken from them without their consent."

During the next quarter-century, this policy was on the whole adhered to.

The rivalries of England, France and Spain . . . [to quote from *The Background of Present-Day Indian Policy,* prepared by the Office of Indian Affairs in 1938] gave the various Indian tribes positions of strategic power... [and]

[4] From "U.S. Government Policy Towards American Indians; a Few Basic Facts; Revised to October 1, 1956." Mimeographed. National Congress of American Indians. 1346 Connecticut Avenue. Washington 6, D.C. 1956. p 1-11. Reprinted by permission.

negotiations with these tribes were carried on . . . on the basis of international treaties. [But] after the cession of Louisiana by France in 1803, the termination of the war with Great Britain in 1814, and the cession of Florida by Spain in 1819, there developed an increasing tendency to deny the sovereignty of Indian tribes and to deal with them by force of arms.

With each new accession of territory, the Government renewed its efforts to push the Indians into the "unoccupied lands" just acquired, and by 1830 a "permanent Indian policy" had been evolved. The Great Plains were to be a vast reservation where the Indians could live apart from the whites but under the protection of the Federal Government, on land which was to be "forever secured and guaranteed to them." When white settlers repeatedly encroached upon these lands, conflict often ensued. Of the Indian Wars which broke out in the 1860's and continued at intervals for some twenty-five years, President Hayes said, in a message to Congress in 1887, "Many, if not most, of our Indian wars have had their origin in broken promises and acts of injustice on our part."

With defeat, the Indians of the Plains lost most of their lands; smaller and smaller tracts were set aside for their occupancy. Indians in other parts of the country were then the more easily persuaded that the only safe course for them would be to submit to life in reservations under the rule of the Indian Bureau.

That rule brought attempts to impose a uniform pattern of administration and of program throughout the Indian country, with little or no regard for tribal differences or respect for Indian customs. Bureau employees were often underpaid and ill-prepared for the responsibilities they carried. Health conditions on the reservations were bad, educational facilities poor or altogether lacking, opportunities to make a decent living conspicuous by their absence. Yet Congress grew impatient because "assimiliation" seemed to be proceeding so slowly—and also because tribal lands were coveted by the whites— and decided to compel the Indians to adopt the white man's way of life, particularly his system of land tenure.

The General Allotment Act [1887] forced the assignment of tribal lands to individual Indians who then became responsible for managing their property and could lease it or, at the end of a specified period during which the land was held in trust for them by the Federal Government, could sell it. Tribal "surplus lands" and lands in heirship status could be sold by the Government at once. When the Indians were given the land in fee simple, that is, without restrictions as to deed rights, the land went on the tax rolls. "The inability of the Indians to keep up with the taxes, unscrupulous practices by the whites, mortgaging of the land to obtain money, and foreclosures, poor management and inexperience in legal matters were among the causes" which led to loss of land. Also, many Indians disposed of their property for a pittance which was soon spent, leaving them landless and impoverished, and most of those who did not sell found their allotments so small and so broken up that they were practically worthless.

Whatever the method, the better land quickly went out of Indian ownership. Between 1887 and 1934, the total of Indian landholdings was reduced from 138 millions of acres to 38 million.

The publication in 1928 of the Meriam report on the administration of Indian affairs revealed a shocking state of poverty, ignorance and ill health among Indians and emphasized the urgent need for a change in government policy. In 1934, Congress authorized such a change. The Indian Reorganization Act stopped the alienation of Indian lands and budgeted funds for the purchase of land for landless Indians. Tribes which *voted to do so* might organize themselves for real though limited self-government and form business corporations for the launching of tribal enterprises. A revolving credit fund was set up and loans for scholarship aid to individuals were promised.

Within the next twenty years, more than three fourths of all the Indians in the United States had *voted* to organize themselves under the IRA; during that time, not one tribe revoked its constitution or surrendered its charter. As of December 30, 1950, corporate business charters had been received by 73 tribes, under the IRA, 15 under the Oklahoma Welfare Act, and 66 under the Alaska Welfare Act. Successful businesses were set up and many Indians gained their first experience in business procedures and in self-government. Each tribe was able to "create its own laws in a wide variety of fields to fit its own special circumstances.". . .

Two measures . . . passed in the hurried concluding days of the first session of the eighty-third Congress, with little or no advance notice and with almost no discussion, established a new policy of the utmost importance to Indians and to the country as a whole.

House Concurrent Resolution 108, passed on August 1, 1953, states:

It is the policy of Congress as rapidly as possible to make the Indians within the territorial limits of the United States subject to the same laws and entitled to the same privileges and responsibilities as are applicable to other citizens . . . upon the release of such [specified tribes] . . . from such disabilities and limitations, all offices of the Bureau of Indian Affairs in [specified localities] should be abolished.

Public Law 280, approved on August 15, 1953, authorizes any state, at its own discretion, to substitute its own civil and criminal code and enforcement machinery for the tribal codes and customs and enforcement machinery, and names five states in which such action is authorized at once, except for specified tribes.

In neither of these measures is there any requirement that the Indians directly affected shall even be consulted, much less be asked to give their consent before the proposed action is taken. Both violate the *principle of consent* approved by Congress in the Indian Reorganization Act.

As required by House Concurrent Resolution 108, the Secretary of the Interior was ready by January 1954, with proposals for the legislation needed to accomplish the purposes of the resolution. Bills providing for the termination of the trusteeship relationship and special services to the tribes named in the Resolution were promptly introduced. They were followed by many additional bills, some ordering "termination" for other tribes, some dealing with other aspects of Indian life, such as "competence," "heirship," and the like—for the most part from an angle unfavorable to Indian welfare.

Thanks to the well-organized opposition of the Indians themselves, ably backed by non-Indian organizations and individuals in and out of Congress, termination legislation was effectively halted except where it allegedly had the support of the tribes affected. Five such termination bills were passed; the others were stopped in committee, as were most of the other bills introduced which would have been harmful to the Indians. However, efforts to get congressional action rescinding House Concurrent Resolution 108 and repealing or amending Public Law 280, although pressed with vigor during 1954, were not successful. . . .

Encouraging changes for the better in the attitude of Congress towards American Indians are evidenced in most of the bills dealing with Indian affairs introduced during 1956. . . .

The principle that government derives its just powers from the consent of the governed has not yet been officially adopted by the United States, so far as its Indian citizens are concerned. A bill which would have recognized this principle, S. 51, after having been passed by the Senate, was "postponed without prejudice" by the House Committee on Interior and Insular Affairs on July 16, 1956. This bill . . . would have amended Public Law 280, Eighty-third Congress, by repealing the section of that law which permits states not already given jurisdiction at will, without necessarily obtaining the consent of the Indians affected. Likewise, no measure to rescind House Concurrent Resolution 108, Eighty-third Congress, was proposed. Unless this resolution is rescinded or superseded by a new official statement of Government policy, such as that in Senate Joint Resolution 85 there will always be danger that sponsors of bills designed to terminate Federal trusteeship over Indian property, prematurely and without the consent of the Indians affected, will claim authorization for their proposals in House Concurrent Resolution 108. . . .

No bills positively harmful to Indians were passed during the second session of the Eighty-fourth Congress (January 3, 1956 through July 27, 1956), and a number of measures were introduced which show a reassuring awareness, on the part of many congressmen, of the real issues at stake and of the policies which must be formulated and adopted if the Federal Government is to act honorably and wisely in dealing with its citizens of Indian descent. . . . Among those of general importance which were passed were the following: Public Law 255 (permits the long-term leasing of Indian land for specified purposes); Public Law 959 (provides for the vocational training of adult Indians living on or near reservations and authorizes appropriations from Federal funds up to $3.5 million annually for this purpose); Public Law 702 (directs the Secretary of the Interior to conduct a survey of Indian education in the United States and Alaska and report findings to Congress); Public Law 715 and Public Law 718 (amends Menominee Termination Act by transferring cost of termination procedures from tribal funds to Federal Government and by providing for wiser planning to protect tribal assets).

RECORD OF THE EIGHTY-FOURTH CONGRESS [5]

The most significant fact about the Indian legislative record of the Eighty-fourth Congress is that not a single bill considered objectionable by the Indians was enacted into law. In fact, few bills objectionable to Indians were introduced. . . .

Only once during the life of the Eighty-fourth Congress did a real crisis situation arise. It came over a bill to extend the life of the Indian Claims Commission. While that bill was under consideration, the Department of Justice made a determined effort to have an amendment added which would have eliminated all claims based on so-called "original Indian title" (aboriginal possession, without grant from a European sovereign or the United States). Indians voiced their strong objections to the proposed amendment and, as a result, it was not even offered on the floor when the bill came up for consideration.

[5] From *Indian Affairs*, newsletter of the American Indian Fund and the Association on American Indian Affairs. no 14. February 1956; no 15: supplement. March 1956; no 18: supplement. September-October 1956. Reprinted by permission.

On the positive side, the Eighty-fourth Congress enacted two bills of major importance to Indians generally. One of them, now Public Law 959, authorizes the appropriation of up to $3.5 million annually for a program of vocational training for adult Indians. It is hoped that as future Congresses follow through by appropriating the funds now authorized, effective steps will be taken to enable Indians to participate as equals in the job market.

The second important new statute is Public Law 767 . . . extending the life of the Indian Claims Commission for another five years without changing any of the basic provisions of the Claim Act. . . . Only a few cases have reached final judgment and have resulted in appropriations. Many more will reach that stage during the next few years. It is hoped that, with the sums made available, it will be possible to inaugurate effective rehabilitation programs for the Indian tribes in question, thus relieving the pressure on the regular funds of the Bureau of Indian Affairs.

Other bills affecting Indians generally, enacted by the Eighty-fourth Congress, include the following:

Public Law 255, authorizing leases of Indian land for a period of up to twenty-five years for public, religious, educational and business purposes and up to ten years for grazing. This makes it possible for Indians to enter into more profitable leasing arrangements than heretofore as the lessees can now place permanent improvements on the leased land and have security of tenure.

Public Law 450, authorizing Indians to obtain mortgage loans on their land, subject to the approval of the Secretary of the Interior. It is hoped that this law will result in improved credit opportunities for Indians.

Public Law 702, directing the Secretary of the Interior to conduct a study of Indian education in the

United States. The usefulness of this law will depend on the caliber of the persons conducting the study.

Public Law 857, authorizing the subsurface storage of oil or gas on restricted Indian land. This law will permit Indians in certain areas to obtain revenue by leasing land for subsurface storage, a purpose previously not specifically authorized.

Public Law 871, makes it a Federal offense to embezzle or steal from an Indian tribe. Hitherto the Indian Bureau has justified its refusal to turn tribal funds over to tribal officials on the ground that these officials would go unpunished if they stole from the tribe. From now on, however, embezzlement from an Indian tribe will be a crime for Indians as well as non-Indians.

Public Law 991 authorizes the Secretary of the Interior to convey to Indian tribes surplus buildings, including their furnishings, located on tribal land or used in connection with Indian administration. As the Indian Bureau gives up or consolidates some of its functions, federally-owned buildings become surplus. Such buildings may now be turned over to Indian tribes.

The Eighty-fourth Congress enacted termination laws (Public Laws 887, 921 and 943) for three Indian tribes, the Wyandottes, Peorias and Ottawas, all of which are located in northeastern Oklahoma. Each of the tribes has specifically requested such legislation. To be certain that these laws would not serve as precedents, Congressman [Lee] Metcalf [Democrat, Montana], one of the foremost congressional spokesmen for Indian interests, announced on the floor of the House that he would object to the bills, and thus prevent their passage on the Consent Calendar, if it were not for the fact that the Indian tribes concerned had agreed to these bills. . . .

EISENHOWER ADMINISTRATION'S AIMS [6]

There are approximately 400,000 "enrolled" Indians in the United States. These are Indians recognized by their tribes as members. Many good citizens consider them a liability, but these original Americans are one of our nation's greatest potential assets.

The Indian Bureau cost the taxpayers $91,112,400 last fiscal year [1954-55]. There are 11,715 permanent and 1,618 temporary employees in our organization, which is approximately one for every thirty Indians which the Bureau serves. This cost represents a levy on every citizen and every business corporation in America.

Our program calls for making this investment pay real dividends in material and social progress, while progressively moving to take the Government out of the Indian business.

In doing this we can add many Indians to the nation's pool of effective manpower, make better use of Indian lands, and speed the day when the Indian will no longer be an expensive special beneficiary of the Federal Government but a full-fledged United States citizen, who shares both the privileges and responsibilities of citizenship—including, in the latter category, the obligation of paying property taxes.

Many Indians are well assimilated into American community and national life. This is especially true in areas where Indians have long attended public or private schools with non-Indians, voted and held public office, and engaged in business on equality with their neighbors. Good examples of such integration are the Six Nations Indians of New York State, the Five Civi-

[6] From "U.S. Aim: Give Indians a Chance," article by Glenn L. Emmons, United States Commissioner of Indian Affairs. *Nation's Business.* 43:40-42. July 1955. Reprinted by permission.

lized Tribes of Oklahoma, and the Indians living in Wisconsin, Minnesota, and California.

But some 250,000 Indians still live on reservations or in nearby communities. Their lands are held in trust by the Government. The responsibilities which the Bureau of Indian Affairs has today are derived partly from 370 treaties drawn up with tribal leaders long ago and partly from statutes enacted by Congress from the beginning of our government. While a few reservation Indians have good incomes from oil, gas and timber, the majority are poorly housed, without adequate implements for modern farming and without regular incomes.

On some reservations health conditions are deplorable. Tuberculosis in some Indian communities runs eight to ten times as high as the national average. Dysentery—from lack of proper sanitation—is several times as prevalent among Indians on most reservations as among their white neighbors. Flu, pneumonia, and infant mortality take their toll.

I do not believe that Indians are lazy or that they lack ability to make a decent living. The major cause for Indian poverty lies in the nature of their environment: poor and badly neglected lands, rapidly increasing populations and lack of opportunities for full employment.

This Administration, with the cooperation of members of Congress of both parties, is determined to give our first Americans a better break. . . . You cannot apply the same yardstick to the nearly three hundred tribal groups throughout the country. One solution cannot cover all their problems. However, I am convinced that we can and must help these people into the stream of modern progress. . . .

Many tribal leaders are awake to the challenge of modern progress. They are no longer content with the policy of "keeping the Indian an Indian." Especially is this true of younger Indians, many of whom were GI's in World War II or in Korea. They have traveled far and have learned the importance of independence and self-sufficiency. . . .

We are attacking the problem with three major projects:

1. Relocation of Indians in industrial areas.

Many reservations simply cannot support the people on them. When I came to Gallup in 1919, there were about 28,000 Navaho Indians. Today there are about 75,000. Their reservation extends over 15.5 million acres of tribal and allotted land. Yet its arid acres cannot support that many people. Most Navahos are sheep herders. In 1954, to conserve their grazing lands, their herds were reduced. But that neither increases their production nor adds to their incomes. On many other reservations similar conditions prevail.

One answer is to help those who want to leave their reservations and find work. Dillon Myer, my predecessor, started this program of relocation in 1952. Now we operate relocation centers in Chicago, Denver, Los Angeles and Oakland, California. Additional centers are planned for Seattle, Kansas City, and St. Louis. To date [summer 1955] more than six thousand Indians —men and women—have been placed in jobs. . . .

Steadily, the program is drawing into good jobs many who otherwise would be idle. Thus it has a double value. It takes the Indian out of the class of special service beneficiary, and it brings to American industry and labor a new and valuable recruit.

2. Better use of reservation resources.

This is the second prong of our attack upon Indian poverty and idleness. One possibility lies in better use of Indian lands. Irrigation can bring some of these lands

into full productive use. Soil and moisture conservation
can increase crop yield per acre.

In keeping with our policy of progressively getting
the Government out of the Indian business, the program
of guidance to Indian farmers is being gradually shifted
to the Department of Agriculture and the land-grant
colleges. This means that the [Department of Agri-
culture] Extension Service will expand its work to include reservation Indians. . . .

We are also moving in to get many tracts of reservation lands back into the hands of Indians who want to
farm or ranch. At present, few Indians till the soil held
in trust for them. On the Sioux reservation of South
Dakota, only about 40 per cent of Indian land is being
used by Indians. On the Blackfeet and Fort Peck reservations in Montana, the percentage is even less. Many
Indians find it easy to lease their lands to white neighbors and receive rent money through the Bureau. . . .

"Fractionated heirships" offer another problem. Almost half of the 115,000 tracts of allotted land in Federal trusteeship are now owned by two or more heirs
of the original allottees. In many cases, scores of heirs
own a fractionated interest in one tract. As a result,
much Indian land is not being effectively used. Yet the
job of probating these estates, managing the lands and
distributing the proceeds is a tremendous administrative
burden to the Bureau. Reports from the field tell of
payments to heirs of Indian lands down to such small
fractions of the income that the costs of bookkeeping and
making out checks total many times what the payments
are worth.

We are engaged in research to determine the best
ways to keep these lands in Indian ownership and make
them productive. Plans are being considered to permit
tribal members who want to go into the livestock busi-

ness to buy up such allotments and consolidate them into larger and more economic units. Our aim is to give younger Indians a chance they have not had to raise livestock on a truly profitable basis. . . .

3. Developing job opportunities in the home areas.

Besides those Indians who want to relocate in cities and those who want to stay with their soil, all other Indian citizens can and should be brought into our pool of productive labor.

There are today very few industries or other payroll enterprises of the non-farming type around most Indian reservations. Yet these areas hold many promising opportunities for additional economic development.

There are great stands of timber upon some reservations, such as the Klamath in Oregon. There are oil and gas resources for others. Stone and other building materials are available on others, such as the areas of the Navahos, Hopis, Apaches and the Pueblos. There is surplus manpower on most reservations. All this adds up to a challenge to help create new employment and lift standards of living for many Indian families.

But we need accurate information showing just what the possibilities are and where they exist. This calls for practical and realistic surveys made by people of experience in this type of economic analysis. This task is too big for the Government alone. We need help from private organizations and public-spirited citizens.

Accordingly, I have interested some of the country's outstanding private foundations in a series of surveys of Indian communities. Five prominent Americans are serving on a non-profit corporation to receive grants from the foundations to finance the surveys. They are: Daniel T. Beals, chairman of the board, First National Bank, Kansas City, who serves as chairman; Laurence F. Lee, the former president of the Chamber of Commerce of the United States, Jacksonville; Dr. Clyde Kluckhohn of Harvard University; William Given, chairman of the board of American Brakeshoe Company; and Roswell Magill, New York attorney and former Under Secretary of the Treasury.

"We hope that the data assembled will encourage new industries to locate in Indian communities, and thus turn local resources into employment and regular pay checks for Indian families," says Mr. Beals.

Our whole plan of Indian betterment calls for trained workers, whether in cities or towns, on the reservation soil, or in new plants. Illiteracy has long been a roadblock against employment of Indians. Now we have begun a program of education designed to teach every young Indian to speak the language of his country—in addition to any tribal language he may know; gradually to eliminate segregated Indian schools and provide minimum schooling for every Indian youth, and to emphasize training in vocations and skills.

"Every Indian prepared to get and hold a job" is our ambitious, but realistic, purpose.

Hand in hand with this ideal is the constant aim of bringing the Indian into full rights and responsibilities of citizenship. No man or woman, of whatever race, can do his or her best work carrying the brand of racial discrimination. The last Congress eliminated several conditions of inequality by permitting Indians to buy and sell firearms and implements of husbandry as other citizens, and did away with the old prohibition against sale of liquor to Indians off the reservations.

Congress also delegated the enforcement of law and order in Indian communities, long under the Federal Government and tribal courts, to state and local officials in Wisconsin, Minnesota, Nebraska, Oregon, and California. [California rejected the transfer of authority.

—Ed.] The legislation also authorized all other states with Indian populations to assume this jurisdiction by action of their legislatures.

What will the taxpayers gain from this program? An official of North American Aviation, Inc., recently told me that the income taxes paid by the 350 relocated Indians since employment with his firm total more than $24,000. The growth in local industry and trade of all kinds, with the development of resources and more jobs, is incalculable.

Education is one of the biggest single costs of the Indian Bureau. For most reservation children in the past, Federal Indian schools have been necessary. Now we are gradually replacing these with public schools. This will not reduce costs, but with the parallel gradual elimination of trusteeship over Indian lands, those lands will begin to produce state and local taxes, which contribute to education. The same may be said of enforcement of law and order.

Personnel devoted to health services for Indians make up about one-fourth of our Bureau employees. On July 1 this year [1955] this activity will shift to the United States Public Health Service. As with the agricultural guidance, better and more economical service to the Indians will result.

Let me emphasize that our program is planned and will be carried out with strict regard for the rights and the welfare of the Indians. We are dealing with human beings and human values. No Indians will be forced off their reservations. All existing treaty rights granted their ancestors will be carefully respected. Rights to oil and minerals will be fully safeguarded. Older fullbloods and any incompetents will be given special protection.

I am convinced that, whatever progress the Indian makes, all that is good in his tribal culture can be preserved. With equal opportunity for employment the Indian will contribute an even greater share of this rich heritage to the building of a greater America.

"RAID ON THE RESERVATIONS" [7]

From the very beginnings of this nation, the chief issue around which Federal Indian policy has revolved has been, not how to assimilate the Indian nations whose lands we usurped, but how best to transfer Indian lands and resources to non-Indians.

The Cherokee Nation is a good example. The Cherokees were literate in the European sense of the word. By the 1820's they had a written constitution providing for a chief officer, a bicameral legislature, a supreme court, and a code of laws. They had their own alphabet, a newspaper, and eighteen schools; some students went on to college. They maintained an active trade with adjoining states, exporting cotton by boat as far as New Orleans. They had Negro slaves and were considering liberating them. In 1794, they had made a treaty with the United States—a treaty consistently kept by them in the years that followed, and repeatedly broken by the United States.

When Andrew Jackson became President in 1828, the Cherokees held only a remnant of their original lands—seven million acres, mostly mountainous, in the area where Georgia, Tennessee, and North Carolina converge. Their best farm lands had gone to the whites.

Jackson conveniently believed that lands had been reserved by treaty to the Indians only as hunting grounds, and that, once the game was destroyed, they should be made available for white settlement. . . .

[7] From an article by Dorothy Van de Mark, free-lance writer. *Harper's Magazines.* 212:48-53. March 1956. Reprinted by permission.

He shortly put through Congress the Indian Removal Act, which gave him the pleasant duty of "leading" the Eastern tribes to some place west of the Mississippi.

About this time gold was discovered on Cherokee lands. Thousands of white prospectors moved in, and Federal aid to support treaty agreements was denied. Within three years General Winfield Scott moved in with seven thousand troops and a great throng of non-military followers. The Cherokee people were seized without warning and put into concentration camps. White camp followers got their livestock, household goods, and farm tools. Most of their homes were burned. In mid-winter the long trek of the Cherokees west began. Some fourteen thousand left their homeland; more than four thousand died on the way. . . .

While the Indians were dying at the rate of one hundred a day, President Van Buren reported to Congress: "The measures [for Cherokee removal] authorized by Congress at its last session have had the happiest effects. . . . The Cherokees have emigrated without any apparent reluctance." He went on to arrange that the cost of the migration be charged against funds credited to the tribe in the Treasury.

The story of the Cherokees is the story of most eastern tribes. They were moved west to new lands, and they signed new treaties under the Removal Act of 1830 which authorized the President "solemnly to assure the tribe or nation . . . that the United States will forever secure and guarantee . . . the country so exchanged with them."

Then gold was discovered in California in 1848, and the immediate problem became the removal of the Indians from the path of western progress. Less than fifteen years after the "exchange" of lands with the erstwhile eastern tribes, the Kansas-Nebraska bill of

1854 opened to white settlement territory which had been set up by treaty as permanent Indian country.

The management of Indian affairs moved from the War Department to Interior in 1849. The Department of the Interior was the agency of Congress to turn over public lands to individuals at the lowest possible prices, and therefore was well equipped to liquidate the Indians for the same purpose. By all rights, under the policy of total suppression of tribal governments and native religions, the tribes should have died out in the ensuing years. But by the 1880's the indestructible Indians began to show a slow, steady population rise—and they still owned some 238 million acres of land.

By now some aroused citizens realized that powerful exploitive interests working through Federal departments were preying on the Indians by planning to abandon wars and migrations for a new smoke screen called Allotment. . . .

The Allotment Act of February 8, 1887, authorized the President to subdivide any Indian reservation into individual allotments, none over 160 acres, to be assigned to individual Indians. Such tracts could not be sold for twenty-five years, and in the event of death, had to be divided equally among all the heirs. Lands remaining after the parceling-out process were to be purchased by the government and opened to white settlement. The Indians' answer was a dignified petition to Congress from the Five Civilized Tribes (Cherokees, Creeks, Choctaws, Chickasaws and Seminoles):

Our people have not asked for or authorized this [allotment], for the reason that they believe it could do no good and would only result in mischief in our present condition. . . . At least two thirds of the Indian country is suitable only for grazing purposes. No man can afford to live by stock-raising and herding who is restricted to 160 or even 320 acres, especially on lands away from water. . . . The changed individual title would throw the whole of our domain in a few years into the hands of a few persons. In your treaties with us you have agreed that this shall not be done without our consent; we have not asked for it, and we call on you not to violate your pledge with us.

But the pledge was violated. Allotment proceeded with great haste through all the tribes except a few in the Southwest whose lands nobody wanted—yet. In many cases more acreage was declared surplus than was allotted to the Indians, and these so-called surplus lands were immediately bought by the Government for $2.50 an acre and thrown open to white settlement. Indian lands were reduced by 12 million acres in 1890, and by 8 million more in the first nine months of 1891. No one taught the Indians farming, and the allotments were too small for ranching. They had little choice except to lease their allotments to non-Indians and when the twenty-five years had passed, to sell. Time only made the situation worse. Allotments were further broken down by being split into heirship equities; there are records of over one hundred heirs to one 160-acre allotment. By 1933, when the new United States Commissioner of Indian Affairs John Collier ended allotment, the Indians had lost 90 million acres and had leased most of the remainder.

Collier's administration, from 1933 to 1945, refutes the useful fallacy that it is impractical to try to educate Indians. His Reorganization Act of 1934 compelled Congress to recognize the tribes' right to self-government, and this time the tribes were asked whether or not they would accept the act. Those who did could, through further referendum, organize as Federal corporations for tribal economic enterprises, and a revolving loan fund was set up to supply the necessary credit.

Between 1935 and 1949, Indians borrowed from this fund more than $12 million which they invested in every possible type of agricultural and industrial enterprise. Not one tribal corporation which used the fund failed, and uncollectable debts amounted to less than three tenths of one per cent of the $4 million due at the end of 1946.

Today no one talks of allotment, but rather of relocation. House Concurrent Resolution 108 declares it to be the policy of Congress to terminate all Federal responsibility for Indians at the earliest possible date. This is the basic move to transfer Indians and their resources to the states on the fully justified assumption that state governments can be coerced by pressure groups as the Federal Government cannot. . . .

The Termination Bills—six were passed by the Eighty-third Congress in 1954 . . . [several were defeated in later years—Ed.] cut off credit funds and abolish Federal protection for the uneducated groups who still need it. They throw onto the states responsibility for such heretofore federal services as education, welfare, law enforcement, and—far from least—protection and development of Indian resources. Such termination means liquidation of Indian trust property, dispersal of tribal assets, and the end of tribal organization. Significantly, two of the first tribes scheduled for termination were the Menominees of Wisconsin and the Klamaths of Oregon, owners of two of the richest remaining timber stands in the country. The Yakimas declared themselves in favor of the move—an apparent victory for the Indian Bureau. Later it turned out that the Department of the Interior had held up tribal funds payments until the Yakimas agreed to termination. . . .

The Secretary of the Interior . . . has power to declare Indians "competent," to remove the restrictions on their right to sell or lease [See "Bureau's Policy on Land Sales" in Section III, below.] Indians sell their land because of poverty; because of poverty other Indians cannot buy it. So the land continues to pass from Indian ownership—exactly as the promoters of the Allotment Act planned seventy years ago.

The allotments were made without regard to sound land use. Some Indians have key tracts—that is, tracts with water or access to water or access to other allotments—whose sale would reduce the value of neighboring tracts. Since the 1920's a protective policy has been followed, providing that the patents in fee which enable an Indian to sell or lease may be issued only upon showing that the sale or lease "would have no serious adverse effect upon the applicant's family, his land, or the tribe; and that the termination of a trust or restrictions would not destroy or jeopardize a timber unit or grazing area." And millions of dollars of Federal and tribal money have been spent to consolidate these lands into workable grazing or timber-sale units.

Nevertheless, in 1953, the first year of the Eisenhower Administration, 2,527 tracts were removed from trust status—three times the number removed in 1952. In 1954, it was 3,200 tracts totaling more than 500,000 acres. But even this rate is too slow for the land-grabbers. The Indian Bureau is speeding up the process with a new administrative policy: fee patents may now be granted without regard to the effect of the sale of individual land tracts on the whole unit. So may competency certificates and other removals of restrictions. Commissioner Glenn L. Emmons' directive states: "You may approve applications without making prior arrangements for access to other lands remaining in trust status." This makes it possible for the purchaser of a key tract to control the value and use of the rest of the

unit—which will consequently probably pass, rapidly
and at token prices, to non-Indians.

Oscar L. Chapman, former Secretary of the Interior, testifying before Senator Butler's Committee on
tidelands legislation, said that he thought it "would
establish the pattern for the greatest giveaway program
in the history of the world."

He went on, "For years powerful pressure groups
have been attempting to raid various parts of the public
domain. They are now redoubling their efforts."

The raid on Indian lands by the same pressure groups
is well under way. . . .

So long as House Concurrent Resolution 108 is on
the books, the policy of our Government is, and will
continue to be, to terminate its responsibility for Indians
at the earliest possible date. Under this policy a sudden
move at any time could effect the final turnover of remaining Indian lands and resources to non-Indian hands.

The alternative is to rescind Resolution 108 and to
adopt as Federal policy a positive program like the one
proposed by the National Congress of American Indians
[See Section VI, below], a program which would allow
Indians to retain their lands and develop their resources,
and which would, at long last, make good the pledges
of all our broken treaties.

Otherwise the raid on the reservations will shortly
be complete.

OUTLOOK FOR THE INDIANS [8]

An assumption which seems to underlie the basic philosophy of much of the United States approach centers
about the idea that assimilation of the American Indian

[8] From "The American Indian in Transition," by John Provinse, former
Assistant Commissioner of Indian Affairs, and others. *American Anthropologist.*
56:387-94. June 1954. Reprinted by permission.

into the normal stream of American life is inevitable, that Indian tribes and communities will disappear.

There was complete agreement on the part of the discussants [at a Wenner-Gren Foundation Supper Conference at the University of Chicago] that this prediction is unwarranted. Most Indian groups of the United States, after more than one hundred years of Euro-American contact and in spite of strong external pressures, both direct and fortuitous, have not yet become assimilated in the sense of a loss of community identity and the full acceptance of American habits of thought and conduct. No one can expect such group assimilation within any short, predictable time period, say one to four generations. The urge to retain tribal identity is strong and operates powerfully for many Indian groups. It finds support in some of the attitudes and behavior of the general American public, and has been encouraged by Federal policy for the past twenty years. Group feeling and group integrity among the American Indians are as likely to gain strength in the decades ahead as they are to lose it.

On the other hand, we may expect continuing adaptation of the Indian groups to the non-Indian society surrounding them. Modification will occur in Indian material culture, in Indian thought and value systems and in tribal organizational arrangements. But the process of change will be so varied in degree or amount, so selective in type or aspect of cultural feature, and so dependent on social factors of racial prejudice, local attitudes, administrative practices in the larger American society, plus Indian group resistance, that it cannot be taken for granted for any particular group of Indians, much less for all.

Further, the [discussion] group was unanimously of the opinion that forced or coercive assimilation is self-defeating in practice, tending to antagonize and drive underground in the Indian groups those leaders who might otherwise develop constructive and cooperative attitudes toward greater acceptance of non-Indian society. Also the extent of coercion that would have to be applied in order to force assimilation—coercion sufficient to disperse the Indian communities—would not be permitted by the American public. Meanwhile, the current practice of telling Indians that their assimilation is inevitable is probably more deterrent than contributory to adjustive changes, since it gives rise to feelings of anxiety and resistance that lead to rejection of new ideas and institutions. . . .

The general prediction, therefore, is that Indian communities will maintain themselves as cultural islands, more or less well adjusted to or integrated into the American system, at the same time that a growing number of individual Indians will make personal adjustments in the general society. With respect to the communities, therefore, the conference agreed that despite external pressures, and internal change, most of the present identifiable Indian groups residing on reservations (areas long known to them as homelands) will continue indefinitely as distinct social units, preserving their basic values, personality, and Indian way of life, while making continual adjustments, often superficial in nature, to the economic and political demands of the larger society. . . .

It has long been assumed that the most successful planning for development and use of reservation resources is cooperative between Government and the Indian groups. The conferees agreed that all experience supports this view.

It was stressed in discussion that the nature of the Government-Indian relationship, with the Government exercising both authority and guidance, is self-defeating, but that with great administrative skill that contradiction can be somewhat diminished. Failure to consult with the Indian groups and achieve their consent and approval in programs affecting their future welfare and status results in frustration, demoralization and unnecessary delays in obtaining improved Indian-Government working relationships. Indeed, the function of governmental services might be most fruitfully performed if defined as the development of the reservation resources and of the Indians who own them, rather than the management of either of them.

It is suggested by some that there may be a purposeful hesitancy on the part of Government to assist in developing reservation resources in order to influence Indians to leave their reservations. If it exists, such a policy is self-defeating, for the insecurity and sense of abandonment likely to be engendered in the Indians probably results in their "digging in" deeper on the reservation. It may be taken for granted, however, that population pressures on some reservations will make it desirable, or even necessary at times, for some Indians to seek their living elsewhere. Furthermore, some individual Indians will want to find opportunities for a life adjustment away from their reservations, even though reservation resources are relatively plentiful. However, with reasonable planning and effort and the expenditure of reasonable amounts of money, the present reservations, many of them with un- or underdeveloped resources, including labor and skills, can be brought much beyond their present capacity to support the Indian population. . . .

It is sound to assume, on the basis of past performance of several Indian groups, that as adequate skills, techniques and leadership are developed among them,

and as the tribe's economic situation improves and permits, Indians can and will assume responsibility for
financing and operating many community and other services formerly provided by the Government, and in some
cases will eventually be able to assume the entire burden.
Therefore the assumption lying behind the decentraliza-
tion of the Indian Service, providing stronger field staffs
to help Indian communities develop such skills and
leaderships, is probably justified. It does not follow,
however, that the basic problems of Indian affairs administration are predominantly problems of organization
and management, to be solved by constant reorganization
of administrative functions. An important factor in
success is likely to be personnel at all levels who are not
only competent, but understanding of the Indian point
of view, non-authoritarian and "people-oriented." . . .

The administration of peoples is a two-way process
and the way in which any program develops will depend
to some extent on the assumptions of the administered
as well as the assumptions of the administrators. For
example, one of the assumptions of the administration
is that no matter what policy is enacted, it can be put
into operation. To considerable extent this assumption
is true because the Indian makes the assumption that
Indians are powerless to affect decisions concerning their
fate and must accept such decisions as others make.

Below are some Indian assumptions relevant to
American Indian affairs [prepared by Mrs. Ruth Hill
Useem, a Sioux housewife]. . . .

It is worthy of note that most Indian assumptions
are negative, unenthusiastic and fearful—the outlook of
a beaten people. Any policy, and more particularly its
implementation, must reckon with these assumptions:

1. That the Indians in the foreseeable future will
remain a series of separate and identifiable groups de-

spite the fact that some individuals are absorbed into dominant population.

2. That over the years, the Indian can expect no consistency in policies regarding him. No matter what policy is today, tomorrow it will be different—even opposite.

3. That the interests of the dominant society will take precedence over the interests of Indians in any policy decision; Indian interests will be considered only when they coincide or at least do not conflict with "white" interests.

4. That the Indian can do little to affect decisions concerning Indians. Furthermore, those non-Indians who are most sympathetic to Indian interests are individuals who have little power either to make or to influence decisions. Non-Indians occasionally have limited power but whatever is done which is favorable to Indians will soon be wiped out by other interests hostile to Indians.

5. That whatever the policy enacted, the Indian will be told that such policy is "in his best interests" or is "for his own good."

6. That the turning over of Indian affairs to the states is inevitable. Concerning this inevitability there are several assumptions:

   (a) That a state administration is more likely to be hostile to Indians than is the Federal Administration. There is more patterned hostility toward Indians locally.

   (b) That state administrations will be less able to render health and welfare services. . . . Local state governments have fewer resources to run those programs than have the Federal agencies.

(c) That state administrations will be run by
persons with whom the Indians are in direct
competition for land, tax dollars, services, etc.,
and, therefore, even though they may understand the Indian more, they will be less likely
to take Indian interests into account.

7. That the stated goals of a policy may be and
usually are quite different from the consequences of a
policy—with the goals usually being more favorable
to the Indians than the consequences.

8. That some type of government agency should
and will be responsible for Indian affairs. Little thought
is given to exploring nongovernmental alternatives. (To
a considerable extent this assumption is shared by governmental agencies.)

III. LEGAL STATUS AND PROPERTY RIGHTS

EDITOR'S INTRODUCTION

Much of the law governing rights of Indians is a result of a series of court decisions, starting with Chief Justice John Marshal in 1801. These decisions are described in the first article in this section as "the most vigorous defense of the rights of a racial minority that exists within our jurisprudence." The basis of Indian citizenship is next analyzed. Both articles are by the late Professor Felix S. Cohen, who as a solicitor for the Department of the Interior and later as general counsel for the Association on American Indian Affairs, participated in many notable court cases.

The editor of a legal publication describes the Indian system of land tenure and property rights. The Indian Commissioner's directive removing restrictions on the sale of lands by individual Indians is quoted in full. In two succeeding articles, a group of friends of the Indians and a former official of the Indian Bureau criticize this policy. A newspaper editorial warns of haste in conferring on Indians full freedom to deal with their own lands.

The section closes with an account of the procedures for dealing with claims by Indians against the Federal Government, which involve billions of dollars.

LEGAL STATUS OF INDIANS [1]

The train of injustices which the Indian has suffered has again and again led . . . champions of Indian rights to go before the Federal courts to challenge as unlawful

---

[1] From "Indian Rights and the Federal Courts," by Felix S. Cohen, late visiting professor, Yale Law School, and general counsel, Association on American Indian Affairs. *Minnesota Law Review.* 24:145-200. 1940. Reprinted by permission.

particular acts of oppression by Federal and state officials, as well as by private individuals. In the judicial decisions that have come down as a result of these challenges, one finds what is probably the most vigorous defense of the rights of a racial minority that exists within our jurisprudence. . . .

It should be clear at the outset that Indians are citizens of the United States [Act of June 2, 1924], entitled to all the rights which non-Indians may claim under general laws and constitutions. If an Indian is accused of counterfeiting, he is entitled to a jury trial, just as any other citizen. . . . The fact that one of the parties in a case is an Indian does not raise a question of Indian rights. . . .

The right of self-government . . . is the Indian's last defense against bureaucratic oppression; for in a realm where the states are powerless to govern [see "State Jurisdiction," in this section, below] and where Congress, occupied with more pressing national affairs, cannot govern wisely and well, there remains a large no-man's land in which government can emanate only from officials of the Interior Department or from the Indians themselves. Self-government is thus the Indians' only alternative to rule by a Government department.

Indian self-government, the decided cases hold, includes the power of an Indian tribe to adopt and operate under a form of government of the Indians' choosing, to define conditions of tribal membership, to regulate domestic relations of members, to prescribe rules of inheritance, to levy taxes, to regulate property within the jurisdiction of the tribe, to control the conduct of members by municipal legislation, and to administer justice.

The right of self-government is not something granted to the Indians by any act of Congress. It is rather an inherent and original right of the Indian tribes, recognized by courts and legislators, a right of which the Indian tribes never have been deprived. The analysis of this right takes us back to the first governmental contacts between the Federal Government and our Indian tribes.

The nature of these contacts is set forth with lucidity in the classic opinion of Chief Justice Marshall in the case of *Worcester* v. *Georgia*, from which the following excerpts are taken: . . .

> The Indian nations had always been considered as distinct, independent political communities, retaining their original natural rights, as the undisputed possessors of the soil, from time immemorial, with the single exception of that imposed by irresistible power. . . . The very term "nation," so generally applied to them, means "a people distinct from others.". . .
>
> The settled doctrine of the law of nations is that a weaker power does not surrender its independence—its right to self-government—by associating with a stronger, and taking its protection. A weak state, in order to provide for its safety, may place itself under the protection of one more powerful, without stripping itself of the right of government, and ceasing to be a state.

John Marshall's analysis of the basis of Indian self-government in the law of nations has been followed consistently by the courts for more than a hundred years. . . . The doctrine has not always been so highly respected in state courts and by administrative authorities. . . .

The first major test of the principle of Indian self-government following the decision in *Worcester* v. *Georgia* arose in the case *Ex parte Crow Dog*. Crow

Dog was a famous Sioux warrior who found occasion to slay his fellow tribesman Spotted Tail. Crow Dog was tried in a Federal court, found guilty of murder and condemned to death. His attorney sued out a writ of habeas corpus in the Supreme Court, claiming that his client was not amenable to the criminal laws of the United States or of the Dakota Territory, but was governed in his relations with other Indians on reservations purely by tribal law and was responsible only to tribal authorities. This contention was sustained by the Supreme Court in a unanimous opinion. . . .

Within two years Congress had enacted a law making it a Federal crime for one Indian to murder another Indian on an Indian Reservation [Act of June 30, 1834]. . . . There are . . . ten major offenses for which Federal jurisdiction has displaced tribal jurisdiction. . . .

It is important to remember that although Indians are citizens of the states in which they reside, they are immune from state control for actions within their own reservations [except in states to which the Federal Government has handed over jurisdiction—see Section IV, below].

The actual exercise of jurisdiction over criminal cases by tribal courts and tribal councils has frequently been hampered by the interference of Indian Bureau officials who disapproved of the "uncivilized" practices of the Indians and sought to substitute a "civilized" system of "courts of Indian offenses" in which the superintendent of the reservation claimed the right to act as lawmaker, chief of police, prosecutor, witness and court of appeal. This . . . was in force . . . until 1935, when it was superseded by a more liberal system which made the so-called Courts of Indian Offenses responsible to the Indian tribes and terminated the reservation superintendent's power to control proceedings in these courts. . . .

An opinion of the solicitor of the Interior Department . . . sums up the powers of an Indian tribe in the administration of law and order in the following terms:

So long as the complete and independent sovereignty of an Indian tribe was recognized, its criminal jurisdiction, no less than its civil jurisdiction, was that of any sovereign power. It might punish the subjects for offenses against each other or against aliens and for public offenses against the peace and dignity of the tribe. Similarly, it might punish aliens within its jurisdiction according to its own laws and customs. Such jurisdiction continues to this day, save as it has been expressly limited by the acts of a superior government.

Recognition of tribal authority in the administration of justice is found in the statutes of Congress, as well as in the decisions of the Federal courts. . . .

What is even more important than these statutory recognitions of tribal criminal authority is the persistent silence of Congress on the general problem of Indian criminal jurisdiction. There is nothing to justify an alternative to the conclusion that the Indian tribes retain sovereignty and jurisdiction over a vast area of ordinary offenses over which the Federal Government has never presumed to legislate and over which the state governments have not the authority to legislate.

The attempts of the Interior Department to administer a rough-and-ready sort of justice through Courts of Indian Offenses, or directly through superintendents, cannot be held to have impaired tribal authority in the field of law and order. These agencies have been characterized, in the only reported case squarely upholding their legality, as "more educational and disciplinary instrumentalities by which the Government of the United States is endeavoring to improve and elevate the condition of those dependent tribes to whom it sustains the relation of guardian." [*United States* v. *Clapox*]. . . .

The doctrine of Indian tribal sovereignty was tested and confirmed in the field of civil litigation in the case of *Standley* v. *Roberts*. The question arose . . . whether a Federal court might, by injunction, restrain the enforcement of a judgment rendered by the Circuit Court of the Choctaw Nation and confirmed by the Supreme Court of the Choctaw Nation, affecting title to land and rights to rentals within the Choctaw Nation. This issue was resolved in favor of the Choctaw Nation by the Circuit Court of Appeals, and the decision was sustained by the Supreme Court. . . .

Application of tribal law to questions of contract and property rights as well as personal relations, has been sustained consistently by the Federal courts.

In view of a fairly prevalent notion that the conferring of United States citizenship upon Indians lessens the force of tribal laws, it is well to point out that the only legal authority for the view to be found in the Federal cases—the decision in *In re Heff*—has since been explicitly repudiated [*United States* v. *Nice*]. The fallacy of the argument that citizenship is incompatible with tribal jurisdiction is exposed in an opinion of the Attorney General holding that the Choctaw courts had complete jurisdiction over a civil controversy between a Choctaw Indian and an adopted white man. . . .

The doctrine of tribal autonomy first enunciated by Chief Justice Marshall was put to a decisive test in the case of *Talton* v. *Mayes*. Under the legal doctrine of tribal autonomy, the powers of an Indian tribe, not being derived from treaties of the United States nor from statutes enacted by Congress, are not subject to the limitations which the United States Constitution imposes upon the Federal Government. It follows that Indian courts and legislatures may proceed without reference to the many restrictions of substance and procedure which the Federal courts have discovered in the due process clause of the Fifth Amendment, for it has long been held that this clause applies only to agencies of the United States and does not give any specific protection against oppressive acts of states, municipalities, mobs, private corporations, religious orders, or voluntary associations. . . .

The decision in *Talton* v. *Mayes* does not mean that Indian tribes are not subject to the Constitution of the United States. It remains true that an Indian tribe is subject to the Federal Constitution in the same sense that the City of New Orleans, for instance, is subject to the Federal Constitution. The Federal Constitution prohibits slavery absolutely. This absolute prohibition applies to an Indian tribe as well as to a municipal government, and it has been held that slave-holding within an Indian tribe became illegal with the passage of the Thirteenth Amendment. It is, therefore, always pertinent to ask whether an ordinance of a tribe conflicts with the Constitution of the United States. Where, however, the United States Constitution levies particular restraints upon Federal courts or upon Congress, these restraints do not apply to the courts or legislatures of the Indian tribes. Likewise, where the Federal Constitution lays particular restraints upon the states, these restraints are applicable to Indian tribes. . . .

The principle of tribal autonomy implies that questions of membership in an Indian tribe are to be determined in accordance with the laws and customs of the tribe itself, at least wherever Congress has not modified or superseded these laws and customs by special legislation [*Waldron* v. *United States*]. . . .

The Federal cases go so far in the recognition of tribal authority as to hold that the Federal courts themselves may be ousted of jurisdiction where tribal law provides that an intermarried white becomes a member of the tribe and subject to the jurisdiction of the tribe [*Raymond* v. *Raymond*]. . . .

The general power of an Indian tribe to determine its own membership is limited only by congressional enactments which grant property rights associated with tribal membership to specified classes of individuals or which empower the Secretary of the Interior to establish final rolls for designated tribes.

Such statutes, generally speaking, do not destroy the power of the tribe to determine its own membership, although they take from that power some of its pecuniary importance by allowing persons whom the tribe does not recognize as members to receive shares of tribal property and by allowing the Secretary of the Interior to deny a share of such property to others whom the tribe does recognize [*United States ex rel West* v. *Hitchcock*].

The doctrine of tribal self-government implies that where Congress is silent, the descent and distribution of Indian property will be governed by the customs or ordinances of the Indian tribes. . . .

The leading case in which this proposition was tested is the case of *Jones* v. *Mechan*. . . . [With regard to an Indian] "whose tribal organization was still recognized by the government [the Supreme Court held that] the right of inheritance in his land, at the time of his death, was controlled by the laws, usages and customs of the tribe, and not the law of the state of Minnesota, nor by any action of the Secretary of the Interior."

The holding of the Supreme Court in *Jones* v. *Mechan* has never been questioned, but the scope of that decision has been limited on allotted reservations by special statutes governing the probate of wills and the inheritance of real property. . . .

Under this legislation a large part of the tribal jurisdiction with respect to inheritance has been transferred, so far as the allotted reservations are concerned, to the state legislatures and to the Interior Department.

Even on these reservations, however, wills of personal property are subject to the jurisdiction of the tribe. On reservations which have never been allotted, all inheritance of property remains subject to tribal jurisdiction, under the decision of the Supreme Court in *Jones* v. *Mechan.* . . .

That the power to levy taxes . . . is an inherent attribute of tribal sovereignty which continues unless withdrawn or limited by treaty or by act of Congress is a proposition which has never been successfully disputed. . . . [*Buster and Jones* v. *Wright.*] . . .

The proposition that tribal property belongs to the Indian tribes is so plain and self-evident that it would not be worth discussion but for the fact that Congress and the executive occasionally have treated Indian tribal property as if it were a part of the public domain of the Federal Government. Thus Congress has provided for the issuance of mineral leases by the Secretary of the Interior upon unallotted tribal lands in nine specified states, for the sale of timber on tribal lands by the Secretary of the Interior, and for the alienation of tribal land to individual Indians, all without reference to the wishes of the tribe. . . .

The case of *Cherokee Nation* v. *Journeycake* . . . analyzes the respective rights of the Indian tribe and the individual member in tribal property. . . . The Supreme Court . . . quoted with approval the opinion of the Court of Claims to the effect that "powers of absolute ownership" were "lodged in the Cherokee government" [and] declared that individual members of the tribe held interests "limited to a mere occupancy of the tracts set apart for homes, with the right to free use in common

of the unoccupied portion of the reserve, and a right
to share in any future allotment." . . .

It is clear . . . that in the absence of Federal legislation, the domestic relations of members of an Indian
tribe are subject to the unwritten or written laws of the
tribe [*United States* v. *Quiver*]. Federal legislation on
the subject of Indian domestic relations covers only a
few particulars. There is a statute which provides that
the issue of Indian-custom marriage shall in all cases be
deemed legitimate for purposes of inheritance of
allotments. . . .

The question of whether action done in the name of
the tribe is in truth tribal action has been before state
and Federal courts on many occasions, and in every case
the courts have held that the definition of the form of
tribal government is a matter for the decision of the
Indians themselves. . . .

The courts have provided two ways in which an
Indian may meet injustices directed at him as an Indian.
One way is to give up the status that subjects him to
the oppression; if he is a member of an oppressed tribe
he may give up his citizenship in the tribe. The other
way is to attack the oppressive measure itself.

The former alternative is based upon the individual
right of expatriation. The latter is based upon the
right of a racial minority to be immune from racial discrimination. This latter right our Indian population
shares with every other minority group in the United
States, and since all the minority groups that have reason to fear discriminatory legislation make up together
a great majority of our population, the asserted right to
be immune from racial discrimination lies at the heart
of our democratic institutions. . . .

If special legislation governing Indians refers to a
racial group, there is no way in which the individual

Indian can avoid the impact of such laws. If, on the other hand, such laws refer only to persons having a certain social or political status, then, presumably, the oppressed Indian, by changing that status, can escape the force of such legislation. . . . The issue whether the statutes that subject Indians to special treatment refer to a racial group or to a group defined in social and political terms is therefore a poignant issue not only to our 350,000 Indian citizens but as well to the citizens of other races. . . .

The Constitution expressly refers to Indians in two connections. Article I, section 8, confers upon Congress the power to regulate commerce "with the Indian tribes." Article II, section 2, declares that "Indians not taxed" shall not be counted as "free persons" in determining the representation of any state in Congress. An Indian who is not a member of any tribe and who does pay taxes is, therefore, in the same class as a white man, so far as the Constitution itself takes us.

Two other clauses of the Constitution refer indirectly to Indians and provide, by way of addition to the congressional power "to regulate commerce with . . . Indian tribes," two independent sources of congressional power respecting Indian affairs. Article VI provides that "all treaties made, or which shall be made, under the authority of the United States, shall be the supreme law of the land." At the time of the adoption of the Constitution, the United States already had subsisting treaties with various Indian tribes, and continued to make such treaties for almost a century afterwards. Here, again, the Constitution gives the Federal Government power to deal with Indian tribes, and indirectly with the members of those tribes, but no power with respect to Indians who are not affiliated with any tribe. Finally, Article IV, section 3 . . . provides that Congress "shall have power to dispose of and make all needful rules and regulations respecting the territory of other property belonging to the United States." This clause provides a base for a large part of the activities of the Federal Government with respect to Indian reservations and restricted Indian property, but again it gives no authority to govern Indians as a racial group.

In view of these constitutional provisions, we have the right to assume, in the absence of strong evidence to the contrary, that when Congress enacts legislation referring to Indians, it is referring to a group defined in political rather than racial terms, and that one who is an Indian, biologically speaking, may nevertheless be exempt from legislation affecting Indians.

This issue never has been squarely before the United States Supreme Court, but the viewpoint here put forward is confirmed by the only statement the Supreme Court has made upon the question, the dictum of the majority opinion in the Dred Scott Case:

If an Indian should leave his nation or tribe and take up his abode among the white population, he would be entitled to all the rights and privileges which would belong to an emigrant from any other foreign people.

There is one Federal case which squarely raised the question whether Indians can avoid oppression at the hands of the Federal Government [*United States ex rel. Standing Bear* v. *Crook*] . . . .

The right [expatriation] has always been claimed and admitted by our government [the opinion of the Supreme Court stated], and it is now no longer an open question. It can make little difference, then, whether we accord to the Indian tribes a national character or not, as in either case . . . the individual possesses the clear and God-given right to withdraw from his tribe and forever live away from it, as though it had no further existence. . . . Therefore, any declaration, instruction, opinion, order or decision of any officer of the United States which denies, restricts, impairs, or questions the right of expatriation, is declared inconsistent with the fundamental principles of the republic. This declaration must forever settle the question until it is reopened by other legislation upon the same subject.". . .

When the Wheeler-Howard Act of June 18, 1934 [the Indian Reorganization Act] offered to Indian tribes a common road to freedom from Indian Bureau control, the Act was widely misunderstood by the Indians themselves. The idea of an Indian achieving freedom through the removal of property restrictions and the breaking of tribal relations was familiar. The idea of an entire Indian tribe achieving freedom in an organized way through the machinery of constitutions, corporate charters, tribal ordinances, and the transfer of Federal authorities and services to tribal agencies, was new and strange. Tribal government seemed to many Indians to promise only a continuation of "rubber stamp" tribal business committees, hand-picked by local Indian Bureau employees, and shorn of all power except the power to surrender tribal assets.

Consequently, many of the tribes most anxious to achieve freedom from Federal control . . . voted to exempt themselves from the bill that promised tribal self-government, while many other tribes that never had felt themselves greatly oppressed went ahead, under the Wheeler-Howard Act, to establish the machinery of self-government. . . .

Indian property rights are of two types—rights of the tribe and rights of the individual Indian. . . . In so far as these [individual] rights are distinctively Indian they involve two questions: (1) What are the rights of an individual member of an Indian tribe with respect to tribal property? (2) What are the rights of an individual Indian with respect to individual restricted property?

In the case of *Mason* v. *Sams* . . . the court pointed out that the right to take a fish [in the Quintaelt River] was, under the treaty, "a right common to the members of the tribe," that "the fish in . . . this stream do not belong to the state, nor to the United States; but to the Indians of this reservation" and concluded that, in the absence of any tribal agreement, the Commissioner of Indian Affairs had no authority to promulgate the restrictions in question. . . .

From this decision two conclusions may be drawn: (1) that the individual Indian has a right to the use of a fair share of the assets of the tribe; and (2) that the Indian Bureau has no authority, in the absence of tribal agreements, to deprive any member of the tribe of the right to equal participation in tribal assets.

Despite popular impressions to the contrary, the individual Indian has the same right as any other citizen to make contracts, to acquire and dispose of property, and to sue and be sued in the state or Federal courts. The real problem of Indian property rights arises only in connection with restricted Indian property, and more particularly with respect to allotted lands. . . .

The break-up of tribal lands (under the General Allotment Act of 1887) left in the hands of individual Indians pieces of land which, in most instances, the Indian could not profitably utilize, and the Federal Government then stepped back into the picture to administer the pieces. Under this system of property supervision Indians frequently complain that they are allowed no part in the management of their own property and that, in effect, the Government handles Indian property as it handles, let us say, a wild-game refuge—with the well-being of the occupants in mind but without conceding to said occupants any legal rights. . . .

Courts have been asked to decide whether the Indian has any constitutional rights in what was said to be "his" restricted property. . . .

The real significance of the decision in *Choate* v. *Trapp* was the holding that Congress itself could not authorize taxation of [individual] Indian lands after promising the Indians that the land would be tax-exempt. . . . Congress has never again enacted a statute that withdrew from Indian hands property rights lawfully vested, and every piece of proposed legislation that falls within this description is analyzed today in terms of the court's opinion in that case.

INDIAN CITIZENSHIP [2]

The doctrine of Indian wardship arose out of a misunderstanding of Chief Justice Marshall's holding, in 1831, that an Indian tribe was not a foreign nation but was rather a "domestic dependent nation," and that its position towards the United States *resembles* that of a ward to a guardian. The opinion and several later opinions popularized the term *wardship,* and the term soon became a magic word in the mouths and proclamations of Indian agents and Indian Commissioners.

Over the years, any order or command or sale or lease for which no justification could be found in any treaty or act of Congress came to be justified by such officials as an act of "guardianship," and every denial of civil, political, or economic rights to Indians came to be blamed on their alleged "wardship." Under the reign of these magic words nothing Indian was safe. The In-

[2] From "Indians Are Citizens," by Felix S. Cohen, late visiting professor, Yale Law School, and general counsel, Association on American Indian Affairs. *American Indian.* 1:12-22. Summer '44.

dian's hair was cut, his dances were forbidden, his oil lands, timber lands, and grazing lands were disposed of, by Indian agents and Indian Commissioners for whom the magic word "wardship" always made up for any lack of statutory authority.

A . . . confusion that helps to maintain the legend of Indian wardship . . . is the tendency of non-lawyers to confuse two very different relationships—trusteeship and guardianship.

Guardianship is a relation that limits the personal rights of a ward. Trusteeship is a relation that limits the property rights of a trustee and makes the trustee the servant of the trust beneficiary.

As a result of many treaties, statutes, and agreements, much Indian property, both tribal and individual, is held in trust by the United States. In the white man's business world, a "trust" is likely to be a property of great value; the trustee is required to protect the trust property and to turn over all the profits of the enterprise to the beneficiaries of the trust; the trustee has no control over the beneficiary's person. In the Indian's world, the same principles should apply; there is no legal basis for the common view that the Indian Bureau may deal with Indian trust property as if it were the owner thereof, or use such power over lands and funds to control Indian lives and thoughts. . . .

The question whether Indians are wards under Federal guardianship has been squarely raised in a series of test cases, in which the general counsel of the Association on American Indian Affairs has participated. In each case the courts have held that Indians are not wards under guardianship, but on the contrary are full citizens of the United States and of the states wherein they reside, and are entitled to all the rights and privileges of citizenship.

The first [of these test cases] arose in connection with Indian voting in Arizona. A 1928 decision of the Arizona Supreme Court had denied the franchise to reservation Indians on the ground that they were "persons under guardianship." Under the Constitution of Arizona, "persons under guardianship" cannot vote.

In 1948 a new test case was brought by Arizona Indians. On their behalf the argument was put forward that Indians as a class had never been placed under guardianship by any act of Congress or any court decision. Such being the case, popular talk or administrative declarations about wardship or guardianship could not deprive an Indian citizen of his rights of citizenship. The Supreme Court of Arizona unanimously upheld our contention and reversed its twenty-year-old contrary ruling. . .

Justice Levi Udall, for the Arizona Supreme Court, declared:

No superintendent or other official or employee of the United States has custody of the person of the plaintiffs. They are not confined to the reservation and may leave it at any time they so desire. The plaintiffs are under no duty to follow the advice or instructions of any Federal officials in selecting a place to live. The power of the commissioner of Indian Affairs, or of the local superintendent, to decide what people might visit an Indian reservation and meet the Indians thereon was abolished in 1934. . . . The plaintiffs have full and untrammeled right to utilize their own property (except their interest in land or other property to which the Federal government has a trustee's title) as they see fit and to receive and expend income therefrom without Federal interference. A . . . beneficiary of a trust estate who is a white person does not thereby become a person "under guardianship.". . .

We hold that the term "persons under guardianship" has no application to the plaintiffs or to the Federal status of Indians in Arizona as a class.

[In a] California [case involving] the right to equal treatment in relief, San Diego County . . . refused to make welfare payments to reservation Indians, claiming that such persons were wards of the Federal Government. This claim was challenged by the Indians concerned, by the Attorney General of California, and by the Association on American Indian Affairs.

The California Superior Court agreed with our contention that Indians are not under Federal guardianship and that discrimination against reservation Indians in the distribution of county relief is illegal.

Judge Mundo's conclusion, February 3, 1953, in the Superior Court of California in and for the County of San Diego:

. . . The fact that laws are passed for the protection of seamen and Indians, as well as other classes of citizens, does not mean that they become wards in the true sense of the word, nor do these special enactments operate to impair other rights which they enjoy as citizens.

Latest . . . is the suit brought by the state of Arizona against the Federal Security Administration . . . to compel approval of a social security program for joint Federal-State payments to all cripples except those who have "Indian blood" and live "on Indian reservations." The state of Arizona sought to defend the position with the traditional argument that Indians are persons under Federal guardianship.

This position was challenged by the Department of Justice and the Association on American Indian Affairs. The United States District Court for the District of Columbia rejected Arizona's contention and held on February 20, 1953, that any discrimination against Indians in social security is forbidden by the Fourteenth Amendment. . . .

Accepting the logical consequences of this decision, the state of Arizona . . . announced that beginning April 1, 1953, Indians . . . [would] be treated exactly like their white and black neighbors in social security programs for the aged, the blind, and dependent children.

So far as the courts are concerned, these decisions work the final burial of the doctrine of Indian wardship.

By Act of Congress, June 2, 1924, all Indians born within the territorial limits of the United States were declared citizens; two thirds of them had acquired citizenship before that date through treaties and special and general statutes.

INDIAN LAND TENURE [3]

Federal Indian property law strongly tends to recognize that the Indians' right to their land is not a right derived from our Government, but a right which they held prior and maintained subsequent to the discovery of this continent. . . .

Though recognized as far back as a congressional ordinance in 1787, Supreme Court decisions held that Indians could own land without having received a grant from a European king or the United States Government and that Indians were the true owners, both from the public and private viewpoint (*Johnson* v. *M'Intosh* . . . ; *Worcester* v. *Georgia* . . . ; *Cramer* v. *United States* . . . ; *Buttz* v. *Northern Pacific Railroad* . . . ; *United States* v. *Shoshone Tribe*). . . .

Indian land rights were often honored in the breach by both settlers and administrative agencies. Federal court decisions frequently compensated Indians for violations of property rights. However, the real oppor-

[3] From "American Indians: People Without a Future," by Ralph Nader, president, *Harvard Law Record*. *Harvard Law Record*. 22:2-6. April 5, 1956. Reprinted by permission.

tunity for Indians to recover for intrusions on their
lands was not provided until the creation of the Indian
Claims Commission in 1946 enabling tribes to present
claims against the United States without obtaining prior
congressional approval.   Since that time, several tribes
have collected millions of dollars.

The relation of Indian land title vis-à-vis the Federal
Government presents a difficult problem of interpretation
of whether and when Indian rights can prevail over the
sovereign.

Supreme Court holdings range from the statement
that Indian title is "as sacred as the fee simple of the
whites" and any Federal purchase should be based on
Indian consent (*Mitchel* v. *United States* . . .) to the
view that the exclusive power to extinguish original
Indian title by purchase resided in the Federal Government (*Holden* v. *Joy*). . . . The latter view is more in
consonance with the realities of Federal power over
Indian land.   What is undeniably clear is that Indians
can neither alienate individual nor tribal lands without
prior Federal approval—the Federal Government being
the trustee of Indian lands.

The subject of original Indian title came up again
in the recent case of *Tee-Hit-Ton Indians* v. *United
States*.   The court (with Chief Justice Warren and
Justices Douglas and Frankfurter dissenting) held that
only when Indian title has been recognized by treaty or
act of Congress is a taking of land or natural resources
by the Federal Government constitutionally compensable.
Although Tee-Hit-Ton title was not recognized, this decision does not affect the majority of Indian tribes who
have treaty recognition of original title.

The Tee-Hit-Ton holding, however, reveals two significant factors.   Although the general recognition of
original Indian title remains unimpaired for most tribes,

the rights derivative from this basic right are still in a highly unsettled state and are likely to be subject to indeterminable distinctions and interpretations in the future. Even a reasonably clear court attitude cannot be culled from the history of Indian cases regarding the finer meanings of original title.

Second, as the Court noted, the question of Indian title "extinguishment" is to be decided not by the courts, but by Congress *(United States* v. *Santa Fe Pacific Railroad)*. Furthermore, Congress, by terminating, as it already has in some tribes the Government's trustee relationship to Indian land, can, as we shall see, set in motion forces rendering the discussion of original Indian title academic as far as the retention of the tribal land is concerned.

Acknowledgment of the right of Indian tribes to reserve portions of their original domain for themselves was the one thing that made it possible for many Indian tribes to regroup their members and survive as an ethnic group. To most Indians, the reservation is all that stands between him and the spiritual and physical destruction that most non-reservation tribes have undergone. The fact that original Indian title, which played so great a role in the past in preserving Indian land, is again thrown into confusion demonstrates the uncertainty of this legal safeguard.

BUREAU'S POLICY ON LAND SALES [4]

It has been decided, after careful deliberation, to modify and liberalize the policy with respect to granting patents in fee [i.e., to remove land from trusteeship and make it available for sale—Ed.] to competent applicants.

[4] Memorandum issued by Glenn L. Emmons, Commissioner, Bureau of Indian Affairs, Department of Commerce, May 16, 1955, to all Area Directors except Juneau. Mimeographed. The Bureau. Washington 25, D.C. 1955.

The policy as stated in the Indian Affairs Manual, Section 201.01, Chapter 2, Part IV, Volume V is quoted below for ready reference:

.01 *Policy* Patents in fee, Certificates of competency, and orders removing restrictions may be issued upon the written application of adult Indian owners and a showing that the applicant or applicants are competent and capable of managing their own affairs; that approval of the application would be beneficial to the applicant or applicants and would have no serious adverse effect upon the applicant's family, his land, or the tribe; and that the termination of the trust or restrictions would not destroy or jeopardize a timber unit or grazing area.

This policy is now modified by giving recognition to the fact that an individual Indian's right to the ownership of his land in fee simple need not be subordinated to the interests of his tribe nor to the management of the land as a part of a timber or grazing unit. Appropriate changes in Section 201 of the Manual will be made at an early date.

In the administration of this liberalized policy you may approve applications for patents in fee on allotments without making prior arrangements for access to other lands remaining in trust status. You may also give favorable consideration to requests by competent Indians for patents in fee to allotments which are under lease, timber contract, grazing permit or other form of use. In such cases, however, the applicant must be informed that the land is subject to the prior valid use agreement and the contractor or lease holder must be informed of the transaction prior to any change in land status.

In critical cases which may seriously affect the protection and use of Indian lands remaining in trust status, and when in your judgment the application of a competent Indian for a patent in fee should be denied, you should submit the case to this office with your recommendation for an exception to this policy.

OBJECTIONS TO LAND ALIENATION [5]

Both the Federal Government and the Indian tribes . . . have spent millions of dollars in recent years . . . to consolidate their grazing and timber lands. This effort and expenditure is endangered by a change of policy recently stated by the Commissioner of the Bureau of Indian Affairs. . . .

The memorandum . . . makes clear that land held by an individual Indian may now be "fee-patented," irrespective of the detrimental effect . . . on the land of his Indian neighbors or the Indian community of which he is a part.

Indian Bureau policy, until this administration, was at least a brake to the sale of lands that would destroy tribal timber or grazing units. The new policy . . . disregards completely the possibility that a land sale may ruin a valuable tribal timber or grazing unit. It even instructs area directors to disregard the need of preserving access to lands remaining in trust. This policy violates basic principles of land use and conservation.

The change of policy . . . has been adopted without consultation with, let alone the consent of, the Indian peoples—in turn a violation of the promise to consult made by President Eisenhower and reaffirmed as Bureau policy numerous times by Commissioner Emmons.

Indians, out of poverty, have been "fee-patenting" their individual allotments of land, a step necessary to

[5] From "Statement on Indian Land Alienation," by the Association on American Indian Affairs, the Indian Rights Association, the Friends Committee on National Legislation, and the National Congress of American Indians, June 27, 1955. Mimeographed. Association on American Indian Affairs. 48 East 86th Street. New York 28. 1955. p 1-2. Reprinted by permission.

selling it. It has been utterly impossible for other Indians, driven by the same poverty, to buy the land, and so it has gone, and continues to go, out of Indian ownership. The issuance of a fee patent takes the land allotted to an individual Indian out of trust status, removing restrictions as to its sale, lease, or other use and disposition, as well as removing it from the tax-free privilege. Last year, in one year alone, over 500,000 acres were taken out of trust.

Indian individual trust allotments had been carved out of the lands originally owned by the tribes. As the beneficial interest had been given to individual Indians without charge, it has heretofore been the policy of the Government to require that where an individual sells his interest, the results of his action for the tribe had to be considered. In this manner the Government properly discharged its trust obligation toward the tribe.

The policy heretofore followed by the Federal Government was of particular importance where it had proved economically advantageous to join a number of tracts to form a grazing unit or a timber unit. The unit brought the maximum possible income to the group of landowners participating in it. In the case of grazing units non-Indian stockmen would frequently attempt to obtain control by purchasing so-called "key-tracts"— for instance, those having water.

It is the strong opinion of the National Congress of American Indians (an organization composed of Indian tribal and individual members), the Association on American Indian Affairs (a citizen group with a long-standing record of informed concern on Indian matters), the Indian Rights Association (with its tradition of active work in Indian Welfare), and the Friends Committee on National Legislation that the Indian Bureau's new fee-patent policy will do great harm to the over-whelming majority of American Indians living on allotted reservations.

THE LANDLESS INDIAN [6]

In the Dakotas the taking of land from Indian ownership is proceeding at an accelerated rate. The sale of Indian reservation land was authorized by an Act of Congress in 1910. . . .

Of course it is technically true that every sale of Indian land originates with the application of the Indian owner himself. A sale could not be made without the Indian's signature. However, it is equally true that strong pressure is put on the Indian landowner, in most cases, to make him want to sell his land. This pressure is artful, persuasive and almost invariably successful. The only possible curb to the avalanche of sales would be a strong land policy by the Department of the Interior.

The Indian petitions his Superintendent to advertise his land for sale if he, the Indian, is "incompetent," and to grant a patent in fee if he is "competent." It is not at all unusual for the white would-be-purchaser or his attorney to work out an agreement with the Indian in advance, including a banker-like use of the money. The results rarely stack up with the plans, however. Invariably the Indian gets a good price for his land, because land is in demand in Dakota; but just as surely, the Indian must use up the money for living expenses. In a few months it is gone, and the land is gone, together with the income he had been getting previously from leasing it. The Indian will then camp around

[6] From "The Vanishing Homeland," by W. O. Roberts, former director of the Aberdeen, South Dakota, office of the Bureau of Indian Affairs. *Indian Affairs.* no 19:3-4. January 1957. Reprinted by permission.

some town or the Agency, living in a tent or an orange-crate and paper shanty, dependent on relief from the Agency Office. Agency records show that as the Indians' land holdings grow smaller, the relief rolls grow larger.

Tribes are empowered by act of Congress to acquire lands from individual Indians who wish to sell, taking title in the name of the tribe and paying for it from tribal funds. However, the success of this policy, like any other Government program, depends on the attitude of the administrative officers handling it. If a Commissioner favors a policy of withdrawal of Federal supervision of Indian affairs, the best way to accomplish it is through the sale of the Indians' property. Obviously, allowing a tribe to buy land from its individual members is not withdrawal.

Tribal officials in the Dakota country are deeply concerned about the loss of Indian lands. They know that when an individual has sold his land and used up the money he does not stop being an Indian. He simply becomes a landless Indian. The loss of his land adds nothing to his ability or desire to achieve integration into the ways of the white man. He has lost his home and the income he formerly had been enjoying through leasing his land. He feels frustrated, discouraged. Tribal leaders are fully aware that this experience is a severe drawback to the Indian's achievement of any permanent advantage wherever he may then live. The tribal leaders see land, only recently sold to a non-Indian, equipped with a good home, outbuildings, fences and a fine herd of white-face cattle. And they see the Indian, land and money gone, begging for a handout at the Agency office, increasingly dependent on the Government for his very existence. The leaders fear for their people. . . .

The Indians must not, however, be written off. Of course, if they are abandoned by the Government before they can take their place in a community, there is trouble, and it matters little whether the abandonment is by termination of Federal services or by the more subtle means of selling out their homesteads. It should not be assumed that relocation off the reservation of a partially acculturated Indian family solves much, if anything; it merely transfers the same problems to another locality. But there is a way out. The problems of the American Indians with their white neighbors lie in the field of sociology. Education, not politics or expediency, is the answer. . . .

The President has several times indicated his interest in constructive treatment of our American Indians. Public spirited people everywhere throughout the nation want to see justice done. But it is getting late for this in the Dakotas. When the Indians' land is gone, then the problem will no longer be one of integration there, and will become a not very inspiring problem in public relief.

Although thought of by many Americans as "the vanishing race," as a matter of fact the Indians are rapidly increasing in number. It is their homeland that is vanishing.

A WARNING AGAINST HASTY ACTION [7]

The position of a significant part of the American Indian population has become truly precarious. This is particularly so in the Great Plains and in the Northwest, where the key to the situation lies in the rapid sale by individual Indians of their allotted land. According to the Association on American Indian Affairs, which acts as a watchdog in protection of Indian rights, some 1.6 million acres of Indian land have passed out of In-

[7] From "Beam in Our Eye," editorial. New York *Times.* p E8. February 24, 1957. Reprinted by permission.

dian control in the last four years. It is too much to expect that when a pot of gold is held dangling before him in exchange for his few acres an impoverished Indian would refuse to make the sale.

But here is where the United States Government, through the Bureau of Indian Affairs, could and should come in. In order to stabilize tribal economy and, in effect, save the Indians from falling victim to an almost irresistible temptation of immediate gain at the price of future ruin, the Government could discourage such land dispersion and even provide help and credit to tribes wishing to buy up their ancestral land from individual sellers.

Much has been heard about rapid "termination" of Federal responsibility for the Indians, and Congress even passed a resolution encouraging it. As it turns out, that resolution was unwise and it ought to be repealed. The Federal Government cannot escape its deep moral responsibility for America's 450,000 Indians. The Association on American Indian Affairs is behind a "Point Four" program for American Indians, which seems to us an approach infinitely preferable to that which has characterized both Administration and Congress during recent years. There is no sense in trying to pretend that most Indians are ready for immediate integration into the white man's life. They aren't, and they need and deserve the kind of help and protection that only the Federal Government can give them.

"INDIAN CLAIMS" [8]

The Supreme Court [March 12, 1945] in the Northwestern Shoshone case, after denouncing the injustices done to a little band of Shoshone Indians . . . denied

[8] From an article by Felix S. Cohen, late visiting professor, Yale Law School, and general counsel, Association on American Indian Affairs. *American Indian.* 2:3-11. Spring 1945. Reprinted by permission.

them the right to recover for these injustices under a special jurisdictional act passed by Congress in 1929. . . . Chief among the reasons advanced by the justices in defending [their] decision . . . was the myth that whatever wrongs had been committed against these Indians were ancient wrongs committed by our forefathers in the distant past against remote ancestors of the present claimants.

The fact of the matter, in this particular case, was that the wrongs complained of began, so far as the evidence in the record showed, about 1907 and are still being committed. . . .

The first point to note in tracing the background of the Indian claims problem is that long before any white man landed on these shores the Indians were making use of the resources of the entire country, within the limits of a Stone Age technology. The country was pretty well carved up into areas exclusively claimed by the various Indian tribes. There may have been some areas only occasionally or sporadically occupied, and there must have been boundary disputes, as there are today among civilized nations, but on the whole each Indian group knew its own territory and the life of each of its members depended upon an exact knowledge of the boundaries and resources of a particular area. . . .

Notwithstanding the popular myth that our forefathers ruthlessly dispossessed the Indian and refused to recognize his prior rights to the lands of North America, the fact is that through most of North America and particularly throughout the continental United States, the validity of aboriginal titles has been pretty consistently recognized since 1532. This is a rather remarkable fact in the history of contacts between races, and but for this fact we would have no problem of Indian claims. . . . The fact that there is an Indian claims problem today, while it points to the fact that wrongs and injuries have been committed against the Indians, points also to the equally important fact that Indians have always occupied a high and protected position in the law of the land. . . .

The process of white land acquisition is one that has been largely misunderstood and misrepresented. I should be the last to deny that wrongs have been committed in the course of this acquisition of our public domain. But the fact remains that of all the public domain acquired by the United States, approximately 95 per cent was purchased through formal treaty or agreement with Indian tribes and only 5 per cent was acquired in other ways. I have no exact figures on the total amounts paid, but my best guess would be that the sum runs somewhere between $500 million and $1 billion. Certainly we drove some shrewd Yankee bargains, but on the whole the Indian did rather better than Napoleon or the Czar of Russia or the Republic of Mexico in their land transactions with the United States. . . .

Mistakes were made in tracing boundaries. We sometimes bought land from a tribe that did not own it and overlooked the tribe that had a better right. Sometimes our agents were faithless in their trust, and the representatives of the Indian tribes faithless to theirs. Other times the money that was to be given to the Indians in the form of merchandise and services was diverted to other unauthorized purposes. Or, we promised to pay the Indians for the land they sold us if, as, and when we received payments from individual homesteaders, and then the homesteaders never came or we put the land into national parks so that neither we nor the Indians could collect any homestead fees.

If any of these difficulties arose in the course of land transactions between private citizens, resort to the courts would be the natural channel of redress. The United

States, however, as a sovereign, is exempt from suit except in so far as it permits injured parties to bring suit. And this is where the difficulties begin in our problem of Indian claims. On March 3, 1865, Congress enacted a statute which declares that the jurisdiction of the Court of Claims, which is the court that ordinarily handles claims against the United States, "shall not extend to any claim against the Government not pending therein on December 1, 1862, growing out of or dependent on, any treaty stipulation entered into with foreign nations or with the Indian tribes." Whatever justification there may have been for discriminating against the contracts we had made with the original owners of the country in giving the Court of Claims general jurisdiction over contract claims against the Government, the effect of this discrimination has been to inject gross delays into our judicial settlement of treaty claims.

For many years Congress has been enacting special statutes allowing particular Indian tribes to bring suit in the Court of Claims for injuries arising under various treaties and agreements. As of February 1940, Congress had passed special jurisdictional acts under which approximately 175 cases have already been litigated or are in the course of litigation. Out of approximately 100 that went to judgment, 26 resulted in Indian recoveries, and these recoveries amounted to slightly more than $30 million. . . .

The present procedure, while it results in substantial justice in a good many cases, involves a very high administrative outlay. There are three factors particularly that contribute to this high outlay. One is the amount of duplication in the investigative work that is involved in this litigation. In the first instance, the matter is investigated by Indian tribal attorneys, and the cost of this investigation naturally comes out of the ultimate recovery, if any. Most Indian tribal attorneys never do get that expenditure back. Then, when a bill has been drafted, the Interior Department and the Department of Justice conduct extensive investigations to determine whether or not the bill has merit and should be favorably reported. The Congressional Committees do the same thing. This may happen at several successive sessions of Congress. If the Indians are lucky enough to get their bill passed, then the whole process of investigation begins all over again in the Court of Claims. This investigation must be limited to the particular case. A large part of this investigation generally goes to the question of the disposition made by various "gratuity" appropriations, which are commonly deducted from Indian judgments. The same appropriations and the same account books must be scrutinized again and again for each separate case. This involves a considerable delay, during which time interest charges sometimes run against the United States. Finally, if a judgment is rendered and the judgment is unfavorable to the Indians, as happens in three out of four cases, the nature of the judgment is commonly such as to pass the buck back to Congress by pointing to some technical defect in the jurisdictional act which stands in the way of recovery. Then the Indians have to go back to Congress and start the whole process all over again. The result is that what should be an expeditious solution of a dispute, vindicating the just claims of the Indians and the honor of the United States, often turns into a protracted and fruitless expenditure of time, effort, and money. The problem we face is whether this process of redressing Indian grievances cannot be carried out in a more efficient and economical way. . . .

Friends of the Indian have been urging a stream-lined administrative solution of the Indian claims problem through the establishment of a special commission to pass on Indian claims. [An Indian Claims Commission was established in 1946, and in 1956 its existence was extended for five years.—Ed.]

IV. TERMINATION OF THE FEDERAL TRUST

EDITOR'S INTRODUCTION

An editorial research organization reports on the move, launched in 1954, to get the Federal Government "out of the Indian business." A release of the Bureau of Indian Affairs summarizes legislative action in this direction.

A popular magazine editorial asks whether the Indians really want to be freed from Federal supervision. The Chief Justice of Oklahoma, a full-blooded Indian, favors gradual relinquishment of the Federal responsibility. Two white groups warn against haste in terminating trusteeship for all tribes.

Former Commissioner Collier vigorously assails the termination policy. A congressman from a state with a large Indian population adds his voice to the opposition. A Jesuit missionary student commends the trend toward relinquishment of trusteeship.

The closing article in this section emphasizes the need for obtaining the actual assent of specific tribes to any change in their Federal relationship. Mere consultation without genuine consent, it points out, is not enough.

EISENHOWER ADMINISTRATION'S POLICY [1]

Nearly 70,000 American Indians, or one sixth of the nation's Indian population, will come out from under the wing of the Indian Bureau and lose the benefits of its

[1] From "Changing Status of American Indians," article by Helen B. Shaffer, staff member, *Editorial Research Reports*. *Editorial Research Reports*. 1, no20:382-98. May 26, 1954. Reprinted by permission.

welfare program when various bills . . . pending in Congress are enacted. [The Eighty-third Congress passed six of these bills; others were pigeonholed or withdrawn.—Ed.] The . . . bills were introduced to set in motion a new policy whose ultimate goal is complete termination of the Federal Government's historic role of protector of Indian rights and property.

A resolution adopted by Senate and House last summer [1953] declared it to be the policy of Congress "as rapidly as possible to make the Indians . . . of the United States subject to the same laws and entitled to the same privileges and responsibilities as are applicable to other citizens of the United States." Indians have been full citizens since 1924, but lands held in common by members of Indian tribes, and some individual Indian property, are under the trusteeship of the Federal Government. And the Government provides various special services for Indians.

The effect of terminating the federal relationship—first for the tribes covered by the pending bills and later for others if present plans are adhered to—will be to eliminate the reservation as a Government-protected preserve for exclusive Indian use. Other effects of Federal withdrawal will be to dissolve the trusteeship over Indian property and subject that property to taxation; terminate legal recognition of tribal governments; and deny access to the Indian Bureau services.

Under the bills now pending, the Indian tribes will have a choice of keeping tribal property intact under private trusteeship, or a corporate form of management, or of having the property or the proceeds from its sale parceled out by the Secretary of the Interior to individual members of the tribe.

None of the various alternatives seems to have much appeal to the Indians themselves. In fact, they and organizations interested in their welfare oppose plans for early withdrawal of Federal supervision. It is contended that few Indians are prepared to manage their own property, and that some tribes hardly can subsist without government help.

Despite the affluence of a few tribes with valuable land holdings, most Indians are poor. A recent Indian Bureau survey showed that 16,000 families were totally or partially dependent on welfare support, compared with 57,878 self-supporting families. "The picture over wide stretches of Indian country is essentially one of poverty and frustration," according to Indian Commissioner Emmons.

There are 400,000 Indians in the nation. Some 61,000 cannot speak English; nearly as many cannot read and write in any language. Some 26,000 of their children do not attend school. The death rate in communicable and preventable diseases is much higher than for the white population.

Conditions among the tribes slated for early severance from Federal supervision vary. The Klamath Indians of Oregon have an average family income of $4,000, which compares favorably with that of non-Indian neighbors. But the Utah Indians, also covered by one of the bills in Congress, have an average family income one third to one half below that of neighboring white families. Some of the other Indians affected by the bills are dependent on seasonal agricultural work and relief. The poorer groups were deemed ready for the change-over, however, because they were considered adaptable to non-Indian society and because the local community was prepared to extend the same services to Indians as to other citizens.

The National Congress of American Indians and the Association on American Indian Affairs nevertheless contend that the Government has a solemn obligation to continue to help Indians improve their living conditions. Beyond that, they insist the Indian has the right, granted in treaties dating back a century or more, to retain use of his ancestral lands for as long as he wishes, and to maintain his way of life without encroachment of the white population.

STATE JURISDICTION [2]

A . . . major item of legislation that came out of the 1953 congressional session was Public Law No. 280. Basically, Public Law 280 was aimed at the rather confusing situation which prevails in many Indian areas because they lie outside the oridinary jurisdiction of the state courts both in criminal cases and in civil actions. Essentially these Indian areas are islands of Federal or tribal jurisdiction surrounded by lands where normal state jurisdiction is in effect. While this unique pattern has worked fairly well in some areas, in other places it has led to a great many complicated legal problems and has often deprived the Indian people of the kind of effective law enforcement to which they are entitled.

Prior to passage of Public Law 280, the Bureau of Indian Affairs had for several years been discussing this problem rather widely both with the Indian tribes and with the law enforcement officials of the several western and midwestern states. In five of the states— California, Minnesota, Nebraska, Oregon and Wisconsin—the Bureau found that most of the Indian

[2] From "Summary of 1953 Legislation," a release of the United States Bureau of Indian Affairs. The Bureau. Washington 25, D.C. 1954. p 1-2.

tribes and practically all of the state officials involved were agreeable to a transfer which would put the Indian areas clearly under the jurisdiction of the state courts in both criminal and civil matters. Accordingly, a number of bills that would accomplish this purpose were proposed to the Congress by the Department of the Interior and these were eventually consolidated in Public Law 280.

Contrary to the impression which some people seem to have, this law definitely did not turn over to the five states the entire administration of Indian affairs on reservations within their borders. All it did was to give the courts and law enforcement agencies of those states criminal and civil jurisdiction over the Indian areas. . . . Moreover, the jurisdiction given to the states was subject to a number of important limitations . . . designed to preserve the trust protections which now surround Indian property, to maintain for the Indians any treaty rights they may have such as those involving hunting and fishing privileges, and to give full force in civil actions to tribal customs insofar as they are not in conflict with the state laws.

The public controversy about this law was centered primarily around two particular sections which were added to the measure during the latter stages of congressional action. These sections, in effect, authorized any state to assume by proper legislative enactment the same kind of jurisdiction in Indian areas which the law specifically conferred on the five states mentioned. In signing the law, President Eisenhower indicated his concern about these two sections—which would make it possible for a state to assume jurisdiction without even consulting the Indians involved—and urged the Congress to remedy this defect by an appropriate amendment as soon as possible.

INDIAN PLEBISCITE PROPOSED [3]

The Bureau of Indian Affairs is a Federal institution that, in the best paternal fashion, keeps saying with regret that its charges are unfortunately not quite ready to run their own affairs.

Congress has been considering eleven bills that are supposed to change all that. There are two ways of looking at them. One way is to assume that these bills are backed by people who want to get their hands on valuable lands owned by the Indians. The other way, less cynical, is to say that the Indian has outgrown the need for government protection.

There are also several organizations that, for other reasons, do not care much for the proposed legislation. The Association on American Indian Affairs and the New Mexican Association of Indian Affairs are among them. They feel, for instance, that it is wrong to lump all Indians together and not to make allowances for differences in tribal development.

Meanwhile the staff of the Bureau of Indian Affairs produces many good arguments in favor of delaying integrating the Indians with the rest of the nation. No bureaucracy can be expected to connive in its own demise. Such things never happen. We are in favor of doing away with all special Indian legislation as soon as possible—provided the Indians want their freedom. Do they want it?

The first thing, then, is to take a sort of plebiscite among the Indians. But if the Indian Bureau is to handle such a survey, it had better make sure that the questions aren't loaded in favor of a few more hundred years of federally managed Indian affairs.

[3] From "Do the Indians Want to be Free?" *Saturday Evening Post.* 227: 10+. July 31, 1954. Reprinted by permission.

GRADUAL LIQUIDATION URGED [4]

Dealing with Indian problems, the United States has followed policies of extermination, forced migration, isolation, and extreme paternalism, none of which has solved the problem. At one time the Indian Bureau tried, under the Wheeler-Howard Act [Indian Reorganization Act of 1934], to make the Indians "better Indians" by encouraging them to continue their tribal governments and retain their reservation status. Such a policy meant segregation, made the Indian race-conscious, and would continue the Indian problem indefinitely.

I advocate the assimilation of Indians into the general citizenship wherever and whenever such course is feasible. The time is here for the establishment of a planned program for the progressive liquidation of the United States Indian Service.

The Congress, the Indian Bureau, the states with Indian population, and the Indians working together should evolve a plan which will lead the American Indians down the road to independence and complete absorption into general citizenship. This is being accomplished through intermarriage, by migration of Indians away from reservations into the non-Indian communities and by association with non-Indians in the armed forces, war plants, and other industries. The educational contracts being made between the Indian Bureau and the various state departments of education, authorized by the Johnson-O'Malley Act, whereby Indian children attend the public schools with non-Indian children are doing much to achieve this end.

[4] From "Solution: Assimilation," by N. B. Johnson, Cherokee Indian and Vice Chief Justice of Oklahoma Supreme Court, in "Whither the American Indian?" symposium. *Rotarian.* 85:26-9. August 1954. Reprinted by permission.

Today many tribes are possessed of material resources in reservation status which require only additional development and utilization by the Indians in order to provide an adequate standard of living for the tribe. Assistance should come from the Federal Government for the development in the form of either loans or grants, or both, so that Indians may have an opportunity to improve their standards of living and at the same time hasten the day when they will be self-supporting citizens and integrated into the life of the community.

However, a number of unwise bills have been introduced in Congress to terminate Federal supervision of tribes for some of our more depressed or illiterate Indians. One of the tribes included is the Seminole tribe of Florida. Ninety per cent of these Indians are unable to read or write and nearly half their children receive no schooling. Another tribe for whom abandonment of Federal supervision and responsibility is proposed is the Turtle Mountain Chippewas of North Dakota. Their average family income was $500 in 1950 and they are generally submarginal socially and economically.

It would be tragic, indeed, for those Indian tribes if the Federal Government should abruptly withdraw its responsibility and obligations to them. The states in which they live would be unprepared to meet the requirements of education, welfare, health, conservation, and road construction. Immediate relinquishment of Federal responsibility and supervision in such states as New Mexico and particularly Arizona, with more than 60,000 Indians, would place a burden on those states which could not be assumed because of lack of schools, hospitals and other facilities now administered and maintained by the Federal Government for Indians.

Steps are now being taken by the Congress and the Bureau of Indian Affairs for the gradual liquidation of the Indian Service. This cannot be done overnight, but should be realized tribe by tribe, area by area, and state by state, and in carrying out this program the Federal Government should not disregard or forget the obligation to the Indians under its treaties and agreements with them.

Indians in such states as Oklahoma, Minnesota, California and Washington, before too long, should be ready for complete relinquishment of Federal control and supervision.

Such a program can be accomplished or fulfilled only through the cooperation by the Indians and the government in all phases of program operations from the planning stage to the final execution.

It is imperative that Congress, the Bureau of Indian Affairs, the Indians themselves, and the general public work together toward a common objective to provide opportunities in the form of long-range programs which will enable the Indians to make a decent livelihood for their families.

VIEW OF FRIENDS OF INDIANS [5]

In a vague way, most Americans believe that Indians once had a good life, before white men came to this continent, and that the Indians of the United States enjoyed as fully as any people the basic human right to equal opportunity for life, liberty and the pursuit of happiness. Our moral responsibility, to them and to ourselves, is to preserve or restore that opportunity.

[5] From "This Way Lies Freedom," a statement of basic policy of the Association on American Indian Affairs. *American Indian.* 7:1-4. Spring 1956. Reprinted by permission.

Realistically, this cannot be done by trying artificially to return the Indians to their old ways or keeping them as museum pieces, even if the Indians themselves would tolerate this, which they would not. We hold, however, that it should be left to the Indians themselves to integrate themselves at a pace controlled largely by their own readiness to take the necessary steps. . . .

First of all, we must extend to the Indians the principle of government by consent of the governed, laid down in the Declaration of Independence. This principle is acutely important for the Indians, because the courts are unanimously agreed that the Congress has plenary power over Indian affairs, and may legislate in derogation of treaties and other agreements; also, for this small minority the Federal Government administers many of the affairs which for the rest of the population are administered by local governmental units highly responsive to the voters they serve and on whom they depend. . . .

Next, we must give the Indians the opportunities in economy, education, and health that will put them on an equal footing with other Americans. . . . The few tribes that have been allowed to create or carry on their own programs have shown wisdom, initiative, and ability to retain their assets. The principle of consent, in the positive form of Indian participation, of doing things *with,* not *for,* Indians, is vital to economic progress. . . .

Almost unanimously, the tribes insist on maintaining their modern, tribal organizations, just as they insist on a voice in their own affairs, access to their own funds, and continued protection of the remnants of their property through federal trusteeship. In regard to this last, they insist that they are not yet able to hold their property without the benefit of trusteeship, balanced by tribal organizations strong enough to keep a check on the trustee. . . .

All through history the pressures to let the Indians "control their own lands" or "free them" from Bureau control have been, to a degree, the result of outside, non-Indian influences, who want the Indian lands thrown open to them, either by lease or purchase. No administrative action or legislative proposal which affects Indian land can be exempt from scrutiny with this in mind.

The desire of Indian communities to continue as tribes is not merely a matter of pride in their traditions or retention of their ancient rights. It is emphatically not a matter of wanting to stand still. They have proven that united, organized tribes are essential tools of progress. They have learned that as tribes they can protect their property, stand off paternalism, make themselves heard, as they could never do if fractionated or disorganized. Through retention of group identity, also, they can retain native values which they regard as essential to the pursuit of happiness. . . .

Their right to be tribes and, individually, members of tribes, is a right of choice, not a compulsion. There is an equal right in tribes or individuals to choose to terminate their Indian status, limited only by provisions of law to ensure that an individual so choosing actually understands the nature and the results of his choice.

Most tribes recognize that every step of progress they make is a step towards that day when they shall no longer need special status, rights, and services. Then their legal status as Indians should be ended. We cannot tolerate in this country a policy looking towards a permanent, hereditary privileged or dependent class of people.

Termination, when it is due, should be worked out by mutual negotiation and agreement. The exact process in any given case, the disposition of community property, the disbanding of tribal organizations or their continuation in modified, ordinary forms of association such as corporations, incorporated villages or, as has been proposed in some cases, the formation of a county, should be fully worked out with the tribe concerned and with the state in which it resides. The procedure should be democratic, not paternalistic. Measures such as we have seen, to impose termination regardless of tribes' wishes, condition, or requirements, are quite as paternalistic as those designed to hold them in unwilling tutelage.

VIEWS OF MONTANA CITIZENS [6]

Citizens of Montana have discussed termination since the Flathead tribe was threatened with liquidation in 1953. We have held forums, studied testimony and policies for other Indian tribes, particularly House Report 2503 (Eighty-second Congress) and House Report 2680 (Eighty-third Congress). We have also profited from contact with local and visiting Indians.

We protest the termination program, its philosophy, its spirit, its goals and its methods. We refuse to go along with the propaganda language: full citizenship, acculturation, anti-segregation and competency. The last particularly is in bad repute because it has been used often to shame and intimidate Indians. . . .

The Indians agreed to end wars and cede lands to white settlers in exchange for certain inalienable lands and certain services which they could not provide for themselves. . . .

If *mutual agreement* to break the trust contract should be reached, total tribal membership should be

[6] From "Obligation of Federal Trust," by James J. Flaherty, chairman, Montana Committee Against Termination. *Journal of Social Order.* 5:66-68. February 1955. Reprinted by permission.

polled; the consent of the elected tribal governing body should be obtained. Every safeguard should be taken that no clique can fee-patent the whole tribe.

The Federal trust relationship was explicitly acknowledged in House Report 2680:

". . . the manner in which the Bureau of Indian Affairs has fulfilled its obligation of trust as an agency of the Federal Government charged with guardianship of Indian property." Yet people who urge termination ignore this issue. They prefer to retort: "You want to keep the reservations. You want to keep Indians segregated. You want them to keep their culture."

The chain of consequences is an assumption. There is no segregation for Indians on reservations above the Mason-Dixon line. Indian culture will go on wherever Indians live. Look at the one hundred Mohawks in New York City, at Chicago's new city reservation, at the fourth generation Indians on Hill 17 in Great Falls [Montana]. Ultimately the Indians' cultural pattern is their own affair, so long as law is not contravened. . . .

Our citizens' committee respectively calls for a halt to termination programs. We also present some practical suggestions as alternatives.

1. "Study the consequences to date and fix responsibilities"—by Stanley Deck, *Indian Information.*

a. The progress of tribes terminated by the Eighty-third Congress: The Klamaths and Menominees are our samples in this new social planning. They had their own tribal lawyers. It is said that they wanted this new step. They have some of the richest forest lands in the country for a stake. Let us watch and evaluate. Let us wait.

b. Hardships of off-reservation Indians: Many are now caught in difficulties arising from agency paralysis. Don't send the Indians off the reservations to learn "full citizenship" responsibilities from Federal and state officials and county welfare boards. We have nine families of unemployables in Great Falls who are told alternately: "Go back to the reservation" and "Stay where you are." Meantime, their children's hungry faces are not good to see.

c. Exiling Navaho children in the Oregon boarding school at Chemawa. They were required to sign an agreement never to return to the reservation. We protest this assault on the Indian family, this displacement of a people from their homeland.

d. Increase of alcoholism on reservations: Indians were "freed from restrictions of Federal law" to enhance their sense of individual responsibility. Now they are being told, "You've had your chance; we're through with you." . . .

2. "Study attitudes of citizens in Indian states"— By Dr. Catherine Nutterville, clinical psychologist; former president, Montana Conference on Social welfare.

The move for termination of the reservation system is creating immeasurable culture shock among vast numbers of Indians. Insecurities, real and imagined, have long been the Indian's lot. The threat of transition into unknown, unfamiliar responsibilities is aggravated by the fact that most Indians have far to go to acquire what we call "American culture." Whether it is desirable that they ever acquire it may be questioned. Not to be questioned, however, is the fact that these Indians, in their present confused state are not, as individuals or as groups, able to achieve the success and happiness that insures mental health. . . .

3. "Learn from Mexico"—By Dorothy Bohn, chairman, Indian Affairs Committee, Cascade County Community Council.

Shortly after Mexican independence, about a century ago, a "termination" law was enacted in Mexico. It was nobly conceived to break up vast concentrations of wealth and to achieve more equitable distribution of land among peasants. But it also forbade ownership by civil corporations and thus ended the *ejidos* [commons, or public enclosed spaces of land] and tribal-owned land. Families were given parcels of land, but the results to the Indian peasants were disastrous. Having lost their tribal unity, rooted in tribal ownership, they were easy prey for land grabbers. By the end of the century, peasants were landless.

Land reforms were carried out in this century. In his 1940 farewell address, President Cardenas reported that 45,330,119 acres of land had been returned. He established credit systems, irrigation projects, agricultural guidance, schools, the revival of Indian culture and arts. The resurgence of native strength and character was founded on the time-honored principle of the agrarian community.

4. "Learn from Canada"—By James J. Flaherty, former president, Montana Chamber of Commerce.

a. The Blood Indians, related to our Blackfeet, have never yielded an acre of land. They sell its products, but all land is tribally owned—the largest wheat farm in North America. In addition the two thousand Bloods on that reservation own six thousand head of high-grade whiteface steers. The tribe has a cash reserve of $4 million held in trust by the Indian Commissioner but at the disposal of the Tribal Council. There are two schools on the reservation, one Anglican, one Catholic. Many have attained outstanding success as professional men in Canada, Australia and New Zealand.

The men who guide the Bloods are specialists. There is not a whole army of Federal employees at Cardston, the agency headquarters. There is an agent with a small staff. Moreover, relationships are personal throughout. The agent knows each Indian and meets him personally throughout the year.

b. The bulk of our American Indians are still living back in the era of the buffalo and the elk. They remain a defeated people. They are hemmed in, frustrated, bewildered. Today they are handing on this bewilderment to their children.

We cannot set a few bureaucratic policies and clearly formulate them, because we are dealing with human beings. Time itself will terminate the problem, and we shall not do it by marking a day on the calendar. The Indian wants eventually to rehabilitate himself and not to have it done by law and by schedule. There should be no concerted effort, which implies force. We cannot help the Indian by using force. We cannot program imponderables.

SPECIFIC TERMINATION MEASURES [7]

The United States is trustee for Indian properties worth tens of billions of dollars. Further, through treaties and other bilateral compacts, it is trustee over the political, social, and cultural institutions and group enterprises of the several hundred Indian groups. The Administration and Congress are driving toward the destruction of the trusteeship obligation, after a preliminary costly perversion of it, and thereby turning over the Indian properties to whites. In justice it must be stated that the jettisoning of the national obligation toward Indians was begun under Dillon S. Myer, Commissioner of Indian Affairs under [President] Truman.

[7] From "Indian Takeaway," article by John Collier, former United States Commissioner of Indian Affairs. *Nation.* 179:290-1. October 2, 1954. Reprinted by permission.

Since the Eisenhower Administration took over, the process has been expedited almost frantically. . . .

Just before Congress recessed at the end of July 1953, a bill was rushed to passage without hearings on its essential provision. That bill became Public Law 280. Signing it, President Eisenhower lamented it as "most un-Christian" and voiced the hope that a future Congress would amend its—and his—errors. There has been no amendment. This Public Law 280 authorizes any state government, in its own discretion, to substitute its own law for Federal Indian law and its own rules for the Indian tribal codes.

In the session of Congress recently adjourned [Eighty-third Congress, second session], the Interior Department pressed its onset, this time not through an "omnibus" bill but through numerous separate bills purportedly dealing with local situations. An example is Senate bill 2745, now signed by President Eisenhower, directed at the Indians of the Klamath Reservation in Oregon. This law forcibly fee-patents—that is, removes from trusteeship status—all individually owned Klamath lands and authorizes any enrolled Klamath member to force the tribe to sell its corporate holdings in order to buy him out; it also brings to an early end Federal supervision of the immense timber operation of the Klamath forests. Here, for once, the truth came out from the Interior Department—that the termination might result "in abandonment of sustained-yield management presently enforced by the Federal Government" and that "accelerated cutting would result eventually in serious injury to the entire economy of the Klamath basin."

The Klamath action is a massive one, as the comparable Menominee, Wisconsin, action now also made law by President Eisenhower. A law directed toward four "small bands of Utah Indians" will have a statistically infinitesmal effect but is massive as to precedent and policy and representative as to method. These 177 full-blood Paiutes are owners, as groups, of 45,000 acres of poor land believed rich in subsurface oil and minerals. Entitled by law to Federal aid and protection, these Paiutes have not been receiving it, hence the Watkins bill (Senate 2670) provided that hereafter they should not receive Federal aid and protection. Congress and the public were told that these groups had been fully consulted and by implication had indorsed the bill. In fact, all but one of the groups have officially objected to the measure. Search of the hearings and reports reveal nothing regarding the adequacy of consultation. The only endorsement of the bill was wrung from a minority of one of the groups, admittedly counseled by the representative of an oil company which "desired to negotiate a lease without going through the procedure" of competitive bidding. Trivial as well as heartless when locally viewed, this bill, now law, was announced as a model for all termination bills. The Federal legal obligation to scores of thousands of Indians has not been fulfilled; past devastating wrongs—such as those done to the five civilized tribes of Oklahoma—have not been righted; therefore, the Federal Government shall be prohibited by statute from meeting the unmet obligations or righting the unrighted wrongs. . . .

Beginning with Dillon S. Myer as Indian Commissioner in 1950, the ruling purpose, harshly intensified by the present Administration, has been to atomize and suffocate the group life of the tribes—that group life which is their vitality, motivation, and hope—and to prevent the continuance and adaptation of those Indian civilizations which have produced great human beings through hundreds of generations. The present Administration's central method is to destroy the Indian Reorganization Act and the life structure which the Indians have built within its authority. The technique is not to use an omnibus bill but a host of special bills— effective in scattering the opposition—designed to destroy the Reorganization Act [of 1934] and its results tribe by tribe and region by region. A looted Indian estate will be the most apparent result, as it was in the case of the allotment acts of sixty and fifty years ago. A less apparent result will be a looted Indian soul and looted national honor, a United States shamed before the forty million Indians of the hemisphere. These results, except in local cases, have not yet been realized. The American public, if it would, could still forbid their irremediable acomplishment.

PLEA FOR A LONG-RANGE VIEW [8]

Like most members of Congress, I believe that ultimately Indians must be given the management of their affairs. It should be the long-range policy of Congress for the eventual establishment of the American Indian as a full, integrated citizen. So that early in the Eighty-third Congress, when House Concurrent Resolution 108, declaring it to be the policy of Congress that certain Indian tribes "be freed from Federal supervision and control" came up on the consent calendar, I did not object. . . . But I was appalled at the administrative interpretation given to the resolution by the Bureau of Indian Affairs and the Secretary of the Interior, and dismayed at the immediate attempt of some congressional leaders

[8] From "A Story of Two Congresses," address by Representative Lee Metcalf (Democrat, Montana), before Thirteenth Annual Convention, National Congress of American Indians, Salt Lake City, Utah, September 24-28, 1956. Mimeographed. The Congress. 1346 Connecticut Avenue. Washington 6, D.C. 1956. p 1-7. Reprinted by permission.

to use the Resolution . . . as a basis for immediate termination of Federal responsibility and withdrawal of Federal services to various Indian tribes. . . .

The Bureau of Indian Affairs is apparently determined to terminate the various services the Federal Government performs for the Indians, whether the tribes or individual Indians like it or not. Consultation is meaningless when, regardless of the opinion of the person consulted, the course of action is predetermined. This was the case in the series of termination bills proposed in the Eighty-third Congress. . . . In the letter of transmittal [of a bill to terminate the Salish and Kootenal Tribes on the Flathead Reservation in Montana] . . . by Mr. Orme Lewis, Assistant Secretary [of the Interior], the result of consultation is recited as follows:

At a general meeting called for the purpose of discussing the preliminary draft, attended by about 130 adult Flathead Indians, a substantial majority voiced their opposition. The tribal council members voted unanimously against endorsement of the proposed bill, declaring they did not want to accept a terminal bill at this time. They are supported in this position by the tribal attorney and by officials of a missionary group on the reservation.

In spite of this . . . the Secretary of Interior submitted the bill to Congress and requested its passage. . . . The other termination bills are in the same category. . . .

All this adds up to the proposition that the relinquishment of Federal supervision and Federal trusteeship must come about in an orderly manner and as a result of gradual change. Today the Indian desires to take his place in a non-Indian world where he can manage his own property, spend his own money, establish his own business or profession. To achieve this, a tremendous mass of bureaucratic red tape must be broken and certain existing policies eliminated.

In addition, the Indian culture as a unique and peculiarly American institution should be preserved. . . .

The tribal organizations of the various tribes are the stepping stones to the assumption of responsibilities of citizenship outside the tribe. The participation in tribal government is training for participation in state and Federal government. Management of tribal property is giving members of the tribal council invaluable experience in business affairs. . . .

Within the framework of existing agencies, many things could be done to help the Indian. Indian resources are undeveloped or are being exploited by non-Indian groups. . . .

Indians must be given help to develop their own resources and the resources of their reservations. The integrity of the present land holdings is the key to the whole program. The lands and other assets have in the past been allowed to slip out of Indian hands until for years the land base has been too small to support the growing populations. . . . Land sales must be discontinued, and if the policy of issuing fee patents is to continue, the tribes must be given an opportunity to purchase the lands when the individual allottees sell them. This will require an extension of credit, sometimes credit up to 100 per cent of the purchase price. . . . Sustained yield forest operations, land base for cattle and sheep ranching, protection of other tribal assets depend on this. . . .

It is gratifying that Secretary of Interior Seaton . . . [recently] recognized that the congressional and departmental action with respect to one of these tribes, the Klamaths, was too hasty and scheduled a review and reappraisal of the Klamath Termination Program in order to send suggested amendments to the Eighty-fifth Congress. . . .

Commissioner Emmons has been traveling around the country holding meetings with representatives of the various tribes. It is standard operating procedure for him to come before a hand-picked resolution committee and make an innocuous opening address. Then one of his assistants will present a suggested resolution to be adopted after a brief meeting. And frequently such a resolution is adopted as an expression of courtesy to the Commissioner and the high office he holds. In one instance the resolution was amended and when the amended resolution was shown to the Commissioner, who was waiting in another room, he refused to make his closing speech until the resolution was redrafted to the Commissioner's satisfaction. Then the Commissioner comes back in and thanks the group for their expression of confidence in his program and declares that he will take their resolution back to Congress as evidence of Indian support of his policies. . . . I, for one, shall not regard such general resolutions as any indication of consultation or approval. . . . If we are to resolve this problem of ultimate integration of the Indian we must work with them, individuals and their tribal organizations. . . .

In short—we must inaugurate a study of the Indian heritage, and draft legislation to preserve and perpetuate that heritage insofar as it can be preserved in the twentieth century world. We must engender respect for the Indian as an individual and his way of life and seek a basic understanding between our races so that we can mutually trust each other and cooperate for the betterment of our American homeland. We must recognize

that Indians are not an abstract problem to be solved by
legalistic formulas administered by a distant bureaucracy,
but that Indians are people, our people.

FAVORING THE INDIAN BUREAU PROGRAM [9]

Though the Government had admittedly been "dere-
lict" over the years in working out programs to make
Indians able to take care of themselves . . . [Indian Commissioner Glenn L. Emmons] feels that there must be an
effort made to forget past grievances and work together
for the future. . . .

The real disadvantage of the Indian lies in the Bureau's emphasis on "wardship" rather than "trusteeship," and the unhealthy spirit of paternalism that has
resulted. Wardship has been used time and time again
to justify the Bureau's use of Indian property as though
the Bureau itself were the owner, and the use of this
power to control Indian lives and thoughts.

It is because of this emphasis on "paternalism" that
so many of our Indians are not financially independent
and self-reliant today. If the Government had taken a
more realistic view, and emphasized those things which
would help the Indian to help himself, his plight would
not be so sad. . . .

This whole problem has been brought to a crisis by
the Republican desire to terminate all Federal trusteeship over Indian properties. . . .

Fortunately, due to the untiring efforts of Indian
leaders and their friends, very few termination bills
were passed by Congress. . . . However, the whole situation may very well prove to be a blessing in disguise
for most of our American Indians. They are forced to

    [9] From "The Future of the American Indian," article by the Reverend
Thomas E. Connolly, Jesuit missionary student. *Catholic World*. 181:246-51.
July 1955. Reprinted by permission.

get vitally interested in their problems and in possible solutions to them. . . .

At last the Indian Bureau has learned one of the greatest lessons of humanism, that every man, in order to develop fully, must have as much opportunity as possible to think, make decisions, and work out his own future for himself. The Bureau no longer intends to impose development and improvement programs "from above." Now it is encouraging the development of these programs by the Indian people themselves, and thereby is fulfilling the very purpose of government—to make men better. Surely that will be the outcome of the meetings Commissioner Emmons is holding throughout the country—the development of initiative, energy, responsibility, self-respect, and confidence in the Indians themselves. This is striking at the very roots of the problem.

However, all this will be of little avail if the Government refuses to give full approval to the well planned programs of the Indians. Unfortunately it is the Department of the Interior which has the final say on Indian affairs, and unfortunately likewise, this department's main concern for the time being is an immediate reduction of domestic spending. It would like nothing better than to drop all protection for the Indian, and get out of the whole Indian business at once.

Therefore it is up to us voters to give our whole-hearted support to the program of Commissioner Emmons and the Indian tribes. . . . They need our help to make a real success of their reservations—to develop their land and resources, to bring in industry, and to promote better health and educational facilities for their people.

As the economic base of the reservation is thereby raised and strengthened, the tribe itself, under the direction of its duly elected Tribal Council, can incorporate and take over the authority and responsibility of the Bureau.   With this opportunity for self-expression and activity, leaders will rise from within the tribe who will organize and direct the efforts and aspirations.   [See "How to Help the Indians Help Themselves," in Section VI, below.]

As the Government yields the authority by which it has substituted for the Indian's disabilities, that authority will be shouldered by the Indian himself.   His community will emerge as an organized Indian society with civil, political and social institutions impregnated with his own Indian culture.   In time, each tribal reservation can gradually take its place within the whole strata of local, state and national societies within the United States.   The tribe will be one more group, working in its own way, toward the common good of the whole body politic.

In this way, the Indian can maintain his identity and his tribal status.   He can preserve his whole social and cultural inheritance as a basis for strength and unity in his family and community life.   His will be a subculture within the larger American culture, and his reservation a homeland within the larger American homeland.   His communal mode of life, will gradually give way to individual ownership and self-dependence; his habit of living will be changed as he adopts more of the conveniences of modern civilization and undertakes its responsibilities.

Nonetheless, the Indian will retain his Indian outlook —his affection for his family and relations, his generosity, his strong sense of democracy and equality, and his love of the earth and all it brings forth.   He will retain his amazing ability to adapt the products of nature to the daily needs of the people.   Once again, from a revitalized people, workers and artists will arise to express their thoughts and feelings in answer to modern needs and problems.

As Commissioner Emmons points out very definitely in his meetings with reservation representatives, Indian workers prove to be of the very best if they are given an honest chance to show their worth. Such an opportunity will enable the Indian to take the same pride in his future that he has in his past, and that is all he needs in order to survive and to be happy.

CONSENT OF TRIBES SEEN AS THE KEY [10]

Oliver La Farge, president of the Association on American Indian Affairs, in a letter to President Eisenhower . . . commended the President for urging revision of Public Law 280 to provide that police functions over Indians shall not be transferred from Federal to state authorities without consultation with the Indians. Mr. La Farge pointed out that the record of events transpiring since the law was passed "clearly proves consultation is not enough." He asked the President to instruct the Bureau of the Budget and the Secretary of the Interior "to report to the Congress that legislation to provide for Indian consent to the transfer of civil and criminal jurisdiction would not be contrary to the program of the President.". . .

On the issue which determines our entire national policy concerning Indian-white relations, Secretary [of the Interior] McKay said [in reply]:

We must start, I believe with the fact . . . that Indians are citizens and now have the privilege of the ballot in all forty-eight states. This means that they are represented in Congress just as other citizens are and that they have the same rights (which they frequently exercise) of petitioning

[10] From "Consultation or Consent," editorial. *Christian Century.* 73:103-4. January 25, 1956. Reprinted by permission.

the Congress and of stating their views before congressional
committees considering legislation. What you are proposing
—and let us be quite clear about this—is that, over and
above these normal rights of citizenship, the Indians should
also have a special veto power over legislation which might
affect them. No other element in our population (aside from
the President himself) now has such a power and none ever
has had in the history of our country. In short, it seems to
me that the principle of Indian "consent" which you are
arguing so strenuously has most serious constitutional implications. With full respect for the rights and needs of the
Indian people, I believe it would be extremely dangerous to
pick out any segment of the population and arm its members
with authority to frustrate the will of the Congress which
the people have elected.

The principle of consent which is now denied in high
places is cited as a "self-evident" truth in the Declaration
of Independence: "To secure these rights, governments
are instituted among men, deriving their just powers
from the consent of the governed." We believe that the
principle still applies, that it does not contradict the Constitution, and that we shall never witness basic improvement in Indian-white relations until it is explicitly
recognized. The amendment of Public Law 280 would
help. . . . Consultation without the necessity of attaining
consent is at best an empty gesture. At its worst it is a
mask for coercion, which is the opposite of consent.

Some advocates of the Secretary's policy attempt to
reduce the principle of consent to absurdity by asking
whether it would be applied to every drunk and disorderly
person before he is jailed, or to every thief before he is
brought before a court to account for his misdeeds. The
objection . . . reveals an unreadiness to consider persons
in any other than an individual capacity, whereas consent
in relation to the Indian must take into account obligations
undertaken by duly appointed representatives of the

Government of the United States in dealing with recognized representatives of Indian tribes. . . .

When Indians ceded land, it was for such considerations as reservations on which they would be undisturbed, education for their children, rations until they could establish a new mode of life, livestock, seed, tools, and so on. Since the government had received full value for its grants—most of the land in the United States cost the Government less than ten cents an acre—it does not now have the right to compel the Indian to pay again for what he has already bought at a very high price. This he would be doing if he were compelled to pay taxes, just as other citizens do; he rightly objects to paying land taxes.

The Indian is a citizen, and he is represented in Congress, as Secretary McKay says. But the Government has contracted with Indians as tribes, and it has the obligation to carry out its agreements. This does not place the Indian in a different category from other citizens, who also make agreements as corporations or communities. The Government contracts with the United States Steel Company to build a plant to roll out steel for aircraft carriers, for example. The company is encouraged to discharge its patriotic duty by a promise that it will not have to pay taxes on its outlay for blank number of years. If the Congress decides to forget that promise and tax the company, it will discover without delay that the company, like the Indians, will exercise its right of petition for redress of grievances and in every way possible will "veto" the Congress' effort. It will fight the case to the highest court, just as the Indians, with far smaller means, try to do. Both are defending rights gained by membership in a corporate body. One of these rights is to withold consent to injustice.

An Indian may sell his land if he is "competent" and if his sale does not undermine the rights of other Indians.

But when he attempts to sell a "key tract" which has the only water in many miles or which provides the only available access to other land, the tribe has the right and duty to stop the sale or to insist that the tribe has the first claim to buy it. In other words, its rights are violated unless its consent is obtained in a matter affecting the welfare of the group. When the Bureau of Indian Affairs attempted last May to encourage the sale of key tracts, the unanimous objection of the National Congress of American Indians, the Association on American Indian Affairs, the Indian Rights Association on American Indian Affairs, the Indian Rights Association and the **Friends Committee on National Affairs** reasserted the importance of the principle of consent.

It is only right that individuals who are members of an association, group or tribe shall be consulted on decisions affecting the welfare of the group. . . . But the next step beyond that is that the group shall consider the matter in hand and give or withhold its consent, as it understands its duty. The individual member of the group has the obligation to cast his vote as his reason dictates, but then he is obligated to honor his membership in the group by conforming to the will of the majority. It is this majority will that determines consent. It is this that the Government and its representatives are obligated patiently to seek. They have no moral right to act without obtaining such consent, except in emergencies when health or survival is at stake.

It will be objected that honoring the principle of consent will make impossible any action affecting Indian welfare. It may be pointed out that the Indian people are often suspicious of anything the white man proposes, that demagogues play upon their prejudices and paralyze groups so they cannot make decisions, that the level of education is so low that the Indians cannot be brought to understand matters pertaining to their own welfare until the opportunity for decision has passed. Such objections prove that the tempo of Indian life moves more slowly than that of the rest of us; but why not conform to Indian pace for a while? What virtue is there in speed when it produces catastrophes like those which threaten among the Klamaths and the Menominees, whose rich forests are about to be parceled out, with the inevitable consequences of sudden riches, followed by impoverishment and the destruction of a valuable natural resource? Both these tribes were "consulted." In neither case was the principle of consent honored. Congress should have waited until a clear majority gave its consent. If we work to raise the level of education, to prove by compassionate deeds and sustained good will that the demagogues are mistaken in the appraisal of our intentions, to seek consent before acting, both we and the Indians will be the gainers in the long run. . . .

V. THE RELOCATION PROGRAM

EDITOR'S INTRODUCTION

Efforts to assimilate the Indian into the general population by finding jobs and homes for Indian families in industrial centers are recounted by the Bureau of Indian Affairs. A nongovernmental group analyzes the instructions given to supervisors of relocation projects.

The authors of numerous articles on Indian affairs describe the program as an attempt to help the Indian help himself. Two free-lance writers tell how it has worked in Chicago, while another is critical of the operation in Los Angeles.

Finally, there is an over-all analysis of the program by the Association on American Indian Affairs.

INDIAN BUREAU'S STATEMENT [1]

The Bureau of Indian Affairs' voluntary relocation program is designed to assist Indians from reservations to settle in communities away from the reservation, secure permanent employment, and adjust satisfactorily to the new living and working conditions encountered. During fiscal year 1955 approximately 3,461 Indians were assisted to relocate. [For later figures, see "A Survey of the Program," in this section, below.—Ed.]

Of the 3,461 who received relocation assistance, financial assistance to cover all or part of the costs of transportation to the place of relocation and short-term temporary subsistence at destination was provided to 2,415 Indians, in addition to all other relocation services.

[1] From "The Voluntary Relocation Program of the Bureau of Indian Affairs." Processed. The Bureau. Washington 25, D.C. 1956. p 1-2

The remainder of 1,046 financed themselves but were extended all other relocation services including assistance in obtaining employment and housing at point of relocation.

During the fiscal year 1955 field relocation office staffs were in contact with over 3,500 employers. Indians placed in various jobs earned average beginning hourly wages of $1.62 for men and $1.07 for women. Most women were employed on a guaranteed wage, plus piece work rates. Average rates quoted for females do not reflect piece work bonus rates.

Interest in relocation has increased among Indians. This has been stimulated largely by increased awareness of opportunities offered through the program, and by letters and other reports received on the reservations from Indians, who relocated previously, relating their successful experiences. The presence of several thousand Indians already relocated in the Los Angeles and Chicago urban areas has assisted greatly in removing fears of loneliness and homesickness. More applications for relocation have been received during each fiscal year in which the program has been in operation than can be handled with the funds available.

The decision to relocate is optional. If an individual Indian or family group is interested, application is made to the agency relocation officer. This is followed by discussion and arrangements which require time up to a month or two, giving the applicant opportunity to understand what is involved in the plan, and perhaps to reconsider.

Relocatees have been placed in employment with several hundred different employers in diversified industries and, in general, gave good satisfaction as workers. The capabilities of Indian workers are becoming better known and many employers are asking for additional people.

Letters have been received from a number of employers testifying to their satisfaction. This success in adjustment as employees has secured acceptance of Indians as workers in some firms which had never employed Indians before, and has played a big part in the success of the relocation program.

Experience has demonstrated that successful relocation involves much more than securing employment. Relocation offices provide realistic counseling and guidance to relocatees, assistance in securing housing, information concerning community facilities and, when necessary, liaison with churches, schools and appropriate local agencies. It is Bureau policy that Indians who relocate should use established local agencies rather than rely on Bureau staff. Local community groups have cooperated fully and newspapers have given their support to the voluntary relocation program. As a result, a survey made on reservations in November 1954 revealed . . . [that] less than one third of the Indians assisted to relocate during the period July 1, 1952 through June 30, 1954, had returned to live on the reservation. And even some of these have gone out a second time.

In December 1954, a new responsibility was given to the Bureau's branch of relocation—that of developing and activating a program of relocation with vocational training for members of tribes for whom terminal legislation acts have been passed. The new relocation and vocational program was explained to a number of training institutions, and it was, without exception, received with interest and a desire to cooperate. From March 1 through June 30, 1955, agency relocation officers took a total of 170 applications and completed plans for the relocation and vocational training of 113 accepted applicants.

The response of the Indian people to this new program, as well as to the Bureau's older voluntary relocation program, indicates that both are filling an important need in Indian lives, and that through these efforts many Indians are being assisted to achieve the living standards wished for them by people of sympathetic and humane intent.

OPERATING INSTRUCTIONS [2]

The step-by-step accomplishment of a relocation is prescribed in detail in *Indian Affairs Manual* [of the Bureau of Indian Affairs]. A digest of the official instructions follows:

Dissemination of Information. The reservation Relocation Office will publicize information concerning relocation opportunities and employment, including living conditions in the cities to which relocation is encouraged.

Acceptance of Applications. The reservation Relocation Office will accept applications and secure adequate information for family-planning.

Planning Relocation. The reservation Relocation Office will discuss with applicants their particular situation, including their qualifications for relocation and employment, their needs and desires and those of their families. Prospects for employment, costs of living, and living conditions in the city will be reviewed realistically. A tentative plan will be arrived at and, together with other relevant information, forwarded to the Relocation Office in the appropriate city. It is the responsibility of the reservation Relocation Officer to determine whether or not an application for relocation should be recommended favorably.

[2] From "The American Indian Relocation Program," a report by La Verne Madigan, executive director, Association on American Indian Affairs, on the findings of a relocation survey team headed by Dr. Mary H. S. Hayes of the Association staff. The Association. 48 East 86th Street. New York 22. December 1956. p 1-22. Reprinted by permission.

Assistance and Guidance Prior to Departure. After the city Relocation Office has indicated that it will accept an applicant, the reservation Relocation Officer will assist the applicant and his family in making arrangements for departure and will give them guidance for the important change to take place in their way of life.

Indian Participation. The reservation Relocation Officer will interpret the program to the fullest extent possible to tribal governing bodies and will try to develop their cooperation.

Relations with Other Agencies. The reservation Relocation Officer will maintain cooperative relationships with appropriate offices of the state employment service and other public agencies to facilitate full utilization of their services by Indians.

Developing Relocation Opportunities. The city Relocation Office will develop opportunities for relocation, employment and housing and promote community acceptance of Indians. This includes interpretation to labor organizations, housing agencies, welfare agencies and religious agencies.

Information to Reservations. The city Relocation Office will provide to the reservation a continuous flow of information with respect to employment, housing and living conditions.

Acceptance of Applicants. On the basis of relocation plans submitted by the reservation Relocation Officer, city Relocation Officers will determine whether the applicant may be expected to succeed. If the determination is favorable, the city Relocation Officer will schedule an arrival date. Applicants arriving without approved planning must have their eligibility checked before service is given. If an unscheduled applicant has been away from the reservation for more than one year, he shall be considered as having accepted responsibility for making his own way in life and shall not be considered eligible for services other than referral to an appropriate community agency to meet his needs. If an unscheduled applicant's eligibility is established, he will be given the regular relocation services, except that priority in handling will be given to those whose relocations were planned.

Services to New Arrivals. New arrivals will be met at the railroad station when this service has been requested in advance. Otherwise they will be expected to report directly to the city Relocation Office.

Temporary housing will be arranged until the relocatee has regular employment. After he is established in a job, he will be assisted to secure permanent quarters commensurate with his place of employment and income.

Counseling and guidance will be provided to explain community recreational and social resources and to give information concerning appearance, sanitation, costs of living and budgeting.

Intensive employment counseling will be provided and, following it, the Relocation Office will contact employers and refer the relocatee for employment.

Continuing Services. Relocatees will be advised that they are expected to assume the same responsibilities for themselves and utilize the same community resources as do other residents of the city. During the period of adjustment, however, certain services will be provided, including: counseling about any problems the relocatee may wish to discuss; periodic visits to homes (generally limited to the first six months); assistance in securing different employment or housing when necessary; assistance in seeking and utilizing educational facilities.

Discontinuance of Service. It is Bureau policy that Indians who relocate should seek and receive services from established community agencies on the same basis as other residents in the community. The services above, other than informal counseling in the office, should not be available to relocatees after they have established themselves in the community and become eligible for public services. For most relocatees services should not be necessary for longer than a year even though a longer period of residence may be required in some communities to establish legal eligibility for community assistance. An over-all definite time limit on the continuation of services is not being set. However, services beyond one year should be extended only when special circumstances require them for the accomplishment of a permanent relocation.

Financial Assistance. Individuals or family groups determined to be in need of financial help may be given assistance for the following purposes: transportation to the place of relocation; shipment of household goods; subsistence en route and after arrival while the workers are establishing income through employment; physical examinations on reservations where Public Health Service facilities are not available (since a physical examination must be passed before a relocation is approved); tools and equipment for an individual or family head who enters apprenticeship training not later than six months after his arrival at the relocation destination. . . . [Allowances paid to relocatees for four weeks from time of arrival vary from $40 a week for a man and wife to $100 a week for a couple with eight or more children.—Ed.] In addition to the above, the city Relocation Officer may authorize up to three weeks' emergency subsistence to relocatees who have lost their employment through no fault of their own and are not yet eligible for unemployment compensation.

Assistance in connection with relocation shall normally be granted only once.

Records. Among the numerous records concerning every relocatee which are on file in the reservation and city Relocation Offices are the following: Certificate of Physical Examination of Applicant for Services of Branch of Relocation (signed by the examining physician); Indian Family Health Certificate (certifying that each family member is free of contagious disease and serious physical abnormality); Relocation Information Record (containing information obtained by counseling with family on reservation, including education of each member, work history of wage earners, etc.).

"OPERATION RELOCATION" [3]

"Operation Relocation," begun in 1952 under former Commissioner of Indian Affairs Dillon Myer, is developing into a major activity of the Indian Bureau under present Commissioner Glenn L. Emmons. Its purpose is to give a helping hand to Indians who want to leave the reservations to find employment. Some 6,200 of the estimated 245,000 Indians on reservations had been resettled by late 1954 (of whom 2,500 are workers in good jobs), via relocation centers established in Chicago, Denver, Los Angeles and Oakland. Additional centers are being considered for Seattle, St. Louis and Kansas City.

"At long last," says Commissioner Emmons, "we are doing more than keeping the Indian on relief. We are helping him to help himself."

For several weeks last summer we visited reservations —westward from the Dakotas to Oregon, thence southward through California, then east to the great Navaho, Hopi, Apache, Pueblo and other southwestern areas.

---

[3] From "The Indians Are Going to Town," article by O. K. Armstrong and Marjorie Armstrong, free-lance writers. *Reader's Digest.* 66:39-44. January 1955. Reprinted by permission.

Everywhere we saw the tragedy of these twin evils: overpopulation in proportion to resources, and under-employment for men and women anxious to work.

When Kit Carson herded the Navahos into their huge, barren tract in 1868, there were only 7,800 of them. Today there are 71,000. The grazing lands and other resources won't adequately support more than half of this population.

In South Dakota the Indian population has grown from 21,000 in 1930 to 30,000 today—and this is about the proportion of increase in all Indian areas.

A few tribes receive good incomes from their reservations, such as the Klamaths in Oregon from timber and the Arapaho in Wyoming from oil and gas. But the majority of reservations are little better than country slums. Not more than 20 per cent of the Crow Indians of Montana or the Shoshoni-Bannocks in Idaho make a living from their own use of reservation lands. Of the 1,700 families on the Pine Ridge Reservation in South Dakota, only 200 are self-supporting.

We asked Charles F. Miller, chief of the Indian Bureau's Relocation Branch: "Why haven't more Indians left for better jobs on their own?"

"Suppose you had never been very far from home," he responded. "Suppose your land and money were held in trust by the Government, and you feared discrimination because of your race if you ventured outside. Suppose maybe you had difficulty speaking English. Wouldn't you hesitate to buck a big city looking for work? Well, that's the situation for many reservation Indians."

Success of the relocation program, Mr. Miller feels, is due to three important things: careful selection of applicants, fitting the Indian to the right job, and adjusting him and his family to the new community.

On each reservation a relocation officer makes contact with those who show an interest in resettling. An applicant must be eighteen years old or more, in good health and of satisfactory reputation. His fare is paid to the relocation center of his choice, and the center pays his living expenses until he receives his first full pay check. He is told plainly that he will be expected to stand on his own feet after he gets the job.

At the Relocation Office, expert interviewers discuss his experience, ability and interests, take him to visit plants and places of business where jobs are available, help him choose. Housing is found for him—and his family, if he has one. Employees of the Relocation Office follow through with help on getting the children into school, how to shop at department stores and super-markets. A minister or priest of the family's faith may call and add his words of welcome.

Several big industrial firms give the relocatees on-the-job training. Many of the Indians attend night school, and the Indian Bureau is now emphasizing manual and vocational training on the reservations.

Why the big cities for Indian workers? Why not small towns near home? Relocation officers give three reasons:

First, unhappily, the greatest discrimination against Indians exists in non-Indian communities near the reservations. But in big cities Indians are readily accepted into school, church and community life.

Second, there are more job possibilities in the cities. Mary Nan Gamble, director of the Los Angeles Relocation Office, pointed out: "Every sort of industry, big and little, is located here. We have 1,000 contacts with potential employers in our files, and 375 have already accepted Indian workers. We hope to double those figures in another year."

Third reason is suitability of Indians for industrial occupations. Says Brice Lay, Relocation Director at Oakland: "With proper training, an Indian can learn to do almost anything skillfully. Our underemployed Indians constitute the most needless waste of human resources in America. For these people the relocation program comes as a rainbow of hope."

From many Indians working at their jobs, and from their employers, we learned how bright that rainbow can be. The Stewart Warner Corporation of Chicago has employed about thirty relocatees. "Indians make good workers," Burt Muldoon, personnel director, told us. "We start them at $1.40 per hour, and after a year many have reached $1.80. Our machines work fast, but nothing is too fast for a well-trained Indian."

Because of the good record made by several Indian employees, the Boeing Airplane Company in Seattle plans to lure more Indians when that city's Relocation Office opens. North American Aviation, Los Angeles, has employed two hundred resettled Indians, finds them particularly skillful at cutting, shaping and riveting sheet metal. "They are intelligent, industrious people," J. M. Wright, employment supervisor, declared. "We plan to continue participating in the program."

Employers are discovering how adept Indian women are as stenographers and machine operators. (About one fourth of all relocated workers are women.) Betty Koester, personnel director of Swimwear, Inc., . . . in Los Angeles . . . walked with us down long rows of sewing machines. Of the two hundred employees, thirty-two were relocated Indian girls. "Navahos, Pueblos, Utes —we like them all," she said. "They are neat, diligent and skillful."

Relocation has a strong appeal to younger Indians. The largest group of relocatees is composed of former

GI's from twenty-eight to thirty-three years old, married, with one or two children. With quiet earnestness, Benny Bearskin, a Winnebago whom we met in Chicago, expressed sentiments we heard echoed by many other young Indians. "They've kept the old folks as museum pieces, through ignorance and idleness, but we young Indians are going to free ourselves by education and work. We can be good Americans, making a decent living, and still keep our Indian culture."

Visiting the Indians, we saw a normal and happy integration into the community. Several were buying their own homes. There were school books for children of parents who never went beyond the third grade in reservation schools. There were radios and television sets.

Indian centers in Chicago and Los Angeles provide a clubhouse with reading rooms, kitchen for refreshments, and recreation hall. They are usually open day and evening, and every Indian in town is invited to come in and get acquainted with members of all the tribes represented in the city. The Chicago All-Tribes American Indian Center sponsors a baseball team, appropriately called the Braves. Its news sheet, *Tom Tom Echoes,* keeps all tribes informed of Indian doings. Teen-age parties are lively affairs. Hearts are never lonely at the Indian Center. Many romances blossom.

In Chicago, the center's chieftain is Ted White, whose father was Sioux and mother Oneida. Winnebago Benny Bearskin helps him with dances and pageants. "We do what the Government can't do—we make them feel at home," White told us.

Not all relocatees are readily adjusted. About 30 per cent go back to the reservations—mostly because of homesickness. But after seeing the folks an increasing number leave home a second time. Steady work and

regular pay have a strong pull. Those who return usually bring a list of names of "relatives" (meaning good
friends) whom they want relocated *pronto*.

Average cost of relocating an Indian worker in all
areas is about $200. "The best investment the Indian
Bureau ever made, both in money and in human values,"
Mr. Miller calls it. He showed us reports on Indians
who had worked at their new jobs for a year or
longer. . . .

As the relocation program progresses, the existing
reservations can better support those Indians who desire to live close to the soil on farm or ranch. The
others can find their places in new homes and chosen occupations, and the stream of a truly noble race, so long
dammed by tradition and prejudice, will strengthen the
current of American life.

HOW IT WORKS IN CHICAGO [4]

The relocation program [in Chicago] grew gradually out of a 1947 attempt to relieve the plight of the
Navaho Indians by finding them temporary agricultural
and railroad jobs.

A Bureau of Indian Affairs office was set up on the
south fringe of the Loop in November 1951. Kurt
Dreifuss, who had been in employment counseling and
rehabilitation work in Chicago, for thirty years, was
named relocation officer. His staff of specialists in housing, welfare and employment today includes eight pro-
fessionals, in addition to Dreifuss and three Indian
clerks.

The first few relocatees arrived in January 1952,
after BIA representatives on the reservations had spread

[4] From "New Deal for America's Indians," article by Madelon Golden and
Lucia Carter, free-lance writers. *Coronet.* 38:74-6. October 1955. Copyright
by Esquire, Inc., 1955. Reprinted by permission.

word of the new opportunity. The program, they explained, included transportation to Chicago and subsistence expenses—$30 a week for a worker and $10 for each dependent—for four weeks, until the first pay check came in.

Many of the relocatees had quit school in the elementary grades and their only previous experience has been in temporary odd jobs or seasonal work on railroads, farms and ranches. So they frequently start as unskilled laborers—assemblers, material handlers, hospital orderlies, and stevedores. However, some are learning trades or qualifying for promotions on the job.

There are more jobs than places to live in Chicago. However, one-bedroom and two-bedroom furnished apartments are plentiful and to the Indians, used to living in cabins and mud huts, anything more than one room looks spacious.

To a woman who has been keeping house under such primitive conditions, even an outdated gas range represents luxury. Often, it is their first encounter with running water.

For the Indian, adjustment to Chicago is often more difficult than for immigrants from other countries. He has been suddenly transplanted from the protective paternalism of the reservation, leaving behind an isolated pattern of living established centuries ago.

In situations of distress, the Indian often remains proudly silent. One relocatee was "lost" in his room for twenty-four hours. He had lost the BIA address. And although he had the phone number he was "ashamed" to ask how to dial.

A common complaint is about the noise, tension and speed of city life. Many Indians climb the stairs to Dreifuss's fifth-floor office rather than tackle that fearful contraption—the elevator.

For women, the restriction of an apartment is especially depressing. Some have locked themselves in their rooms, afraid to go out and tackle the supermarkets.

"But as long as we have good jobs, we're going to stay," an ex-GI from New Mexico says. "Our children have a chance here."

The subtleties cause even more trouble in the long run than the physical aspects of city living.

"You were taught to resist high-pressure salesmanship. Most of us never heard of it until we got taken," lamented a Zuni who had bought a car and TV set on the installment plan, and had lost both possessions and money when he couldn't meet the payments.

Probably typical of the Indians who have made the grade in Chicago is a Hopi who discovered that his ill health was a result of poor diet, corrected the condition and is now a key man on the assembly line.

The relocation program, of course, is not the answer for every Indian who tries it. So far, about two thirds of those who have come to Chicago are still employed there or in other urban centers. Recently the BIA office reported that of some 3,000 Indians who had come to Chicago under the program, about 2,000 were still there. Of the others, roughly 800 had returned to their reservations and about 400 had struck out on their own.

The Bureau estimates that income taxes now being paid by relocatees earning steady wages for the first time have, alone, largely repaid Government investment in resettlement.

There is no doubt of the success of the Chicago experiment. True, the present generation of relocated Indians, handicapped by lack of education and unfamiliarity with urban culture, fill the lesser jobs, live in the lesser neighborhoods. But the overwhelming majority are doubtlessly better off from every angle. Their children, of course, will make the great gains and flow more easily into their rightful place in the mainstream of American life.

UPROOTING THE INDIANS [5]

The Relocation Program being carried out by the Bureau of Indian Affairs was established in 1951 to help the Indians become part of the national economy and part of the national life. However, it did not really become important until August 15, 1953, when President Eisenhower signed Public Law 280. That law, which he branded as "most un-Christian," authorizes any state to substitute its own law for Federal Indian law and its own codes for Indian tribal codes. It was enthusiastically hailed in the Western states by persons who had long been seeking legal sanction to move in on Indian lands, superficially poor but rich in subsurface oil and minerals. Further strength was given to the program to dislodge the Indians under the terms of the Watkins Bill (Senate 2670), providing that the 177 pure-blood Paiutes who own 45,000 acres of potentially valuable land in Nevada should no longer receive Federal aid protection. Another precedent to weaken the Indians' hold on their whittled-down grants was set by Senate Bill 2745, which forcibly removed from trusteeship status all individually owned Klamath lands in Oregon and which authorized any enrolled Klamath to force the tribe to sell its corporate holdings in order to buy him out.

Other bills now pending promise to end all Federal services to Indians, to liquidate all tribal organizations, and to dispose of their holdings.

[5] From article by Ruth Mulvey Harmer, free-lance writer. *Atlantic Monthly.* 197:54-7. March 1956. Reprinted by permission.

However, the Bureau of Indian Affairs is accomplishing that end so rapidly through the Relocation Program that additional laws may be simply *ex post facto* legislative items. A remarkably effective sales campaign is promoting thousands of Indians to abandon their lands and interests for the "promised lands" of the relocation centers.

In defense of the program, an officer of the Bureau of Indian Affairs points out that some of the new immigrants to the urban centers have become model citizens and are "enjoying the fruits of twentieth century civilization . . . up to and including television sets." That is true. But the Bureau is curiously vague about the number of maladjustments and even the number of returnees, which well-informed welfare and social workers in several of the centers set at 60 per cent.

For every success story, there are a hundred failures. For every former trapper-farmer now adjusted to assembly-line work and city life, there are ninety-nine adrift in a new and hostile environment. Against the optimistic pronouncement of government agents that "with a little proper guidance, Indians have no trouble making the major adjustment from reservation to city life" is the bitter cry of Little Light [an Oklahoma Creek] : "So this is the land of sunshine they promised us!"

A damning summary of the program was spoken by a woman in the chairless kitchen-dining-living room of a small shanty on the outskirts of Los Angeles. Five children . . . sheltered against her skirt. The walls were unpainted, the floor a patchwork of linoleum. Through an archway, another room was visible where three beds crowded together. A two-burner gas stove stood on a box, and on the only other piece of furniture in the room—a battered table—rested the remains of dinner—

some white, grease-soaked bags which had contained hamburgers and fried potatoes prepared by the restaurant a few blocks away.

She answered our questions in an Indian dialect which the woman beside me interpreted. "No, my husband is not here. He went out with some other men. He does every night. They are drinking.

"Yes, he is working. He makes lots of money. One dollar and sixty cents an hour in the airplane factory.

"Yes, the children are in school. All but Zena." She indicated one of the girls, about ten years old. "Zena is sick. I don't know what sickness. There is no doctor.

"Yes, the food came from that place. I don't go to the store often. Everybody laughs at me.

"Yes, I want to go back. There is not money. We pay seventy-five dollars a month for this house. We pay for food. We pay for lights. We don't have the money to go back."

Then the patient planes of her face became distorted "They did not tell us it would be like this."

What had "they" told Little Light and her husband?

A good indication may be found in an article entitled "Relocation News" written by George Shubert for the *Fort Berthold Agency and News Bulletin* of Newtown, North Dakota, for May 12, 1953. Following a glowing account of jobs for young men and women with a large company in Chicago—"skilled, lifetime jobs . . . with paid vacation, sick benefits, paid pension plan, union membership, protection, etc."—the Indian Affairs officer wrote:

This office is presently equipped to offer financial assistance to a large number of qualified persons who have an earnest desire to improve their standard of living, by accepting permanent employment and relocation in one of four large urban areas in the United States: namely Chicago, Illinois, Denver, Colorado, Oakland, California (including the entire Bay Area) and Los Angeles, California.

Our offices in those areas are presently able to place on jobs and render any assistance necessary to practically an unlimited number of families. They also state that there is a good selection of employment opportunities and housing facilities available at the present time.

For those who cannot be reached by words, there is the poster recently concocted in the Los Angeles Relocation Center picturing a number of pleasant, comfortable houses owned by Indians who are shown demonstrating the wonders of garbage disposals in the assorted kitchens and of television sets in the assorted living rooms.

The salesmanship rates an A plus, but what about the product?

First of all, the Government's financial assistance in connection with relocation is limited specifically to one-way travel costs and a weekly allowance until the first pay check comes in. Those monetary aids are made only to persons without any funds; partial grants are given to those who have some reserves. But that even the maximum grant is sufficient is highly debatable; transportation costs and a living allowance for a few weeks might be all that a bright young man moving from San Francisco to New York would need to tide him over the transitional period; it is not enough to cover the period of adjustment needed by a family moving from a pre-Columbian culture into the mechanized twentieth century.

"Accepting permanent employment" is another rather meaningless phrase since absolute job security is almost nonexistent. Moreover, many of the Indians find it impossible to work in foundries or at assembly-line jobs after a history of out-door experience. The Bureau of Indian Affairs accepts no responsibility for those who wish to transfer from the jobs they took blind when they first arrived.

That the Relocation Offices in the four areas are presently able to "render any assistances necessary to practically an unlimited number of families" is an absurdity. In Los Angeles, where between 150 and 200 new arrivals are pouring each month under government sponsorship (another 100 are coming on their own), the Relocation Office has a staff of fourteen persons, including clerks, receptionists, secretaries, and others who play no active role in the "integration." Those who do, necessarily confine themselves to receiving the Indians who show up at the office, making job contacts for them, giving them a living allowance and the address of a vacant dwelling.

This sketchy reception is obviously a prologue to disaster for persons whose acquaintance with the American language is painfully new if it exists at all, who are not accustomed to handling money—most of them have lived in an agricultural environment where barter is the approved method of exchange—who are generally more ignorant of urban ways than a six-year-old child reared in a city, and who become unutterably lonely removed from the security of tribal identity.

Their first glimpse of city life is rarely happy. In Los Angeles, where there has been an acute housing shortage since the beginning of World War II, the Indians have been hard pressed to find decent accommodations. Many of them are sent to antiquated rooming houses and apartments in the Bunker Hill area, which is now being razed with Federal and municipal funds. Others are sent to trailer courts and dreary buildings in the southern part of the city near the aircraft plants.

For many, a few days is enough; others leave in a few weeks; some stay, and for most the going is rough.

A number of the men—particularly the GI's and those who have taken the five-year training course at Sherman Institute or other Government schools—fare rather well. They know English, they have learned a trade, they have had an extended relationship with white men and white men's ways. But most are hopeless and dangerous misfits.

The Indians in Los Angeles—and there are now ten thousand of them, representing eighty-six tribes— have had a relatively good police record; a one per cent arrest, mostly on charges of drunken driving and "plain drunk." That figure soared in 1955. . . .

The Los Angeles Indian Center . . . began in 1935, when Myra Bartlett, an Indian, . . . decided to establish a meeting place for the Indian women working as house-maids whom she encountered each Thursday afternoon gathered at the streetcar terminal for a "weekly visit." It was a refugee center during the depression and was reorganized under the American Friends Service Com-mittee in 1948 and supported by that group until last October [1955]. Now on its own with a $20,000 yearly budget and a staff of two persons—Mrs. [Stevie White-face] Standingbear and Mary Buck—the Center has be-come an island of security for the Indians in Los Angeles.

One of its main functions is to make available to newly arrived and needy Indians the help of those estab-lished in the city. More than two hundred volunteers render all kinds of services from baby-sitting and prac-tical nursing to loaning or giving money, finding decent living quarters, obtaining medical treatment, and just visiting.

Aside from this emergency work, the Center pro-vides a familiar environment for the ten thousand In-dians in Los Angeles. Its dances, dinners, classes, clubs and activities for all age groups have an average weekly attendance of more than six hundred. The Center's chapter of Alcoholics Anonymous has rescued scores of men and women. Although the Center itself has little money, it is often able to scrape up a bit to tide destitute persons over a period of immediate want. This is particularly valuable since municipal and state services are not available to persons who have not fulfilled residence requirements. "We can get medical care for some people by taking them—including pregnant women—through the emergency entrance," Stevie Standingbear reports. But those who are not specifically emergency cases must either find a creditor or wait until their sickness becomes acute. A small number obtain some help from one of the professional men and women who aid the Center "as a charity." The courts parole to the Center some of the newer arrivals who have been picked up for drunkenness. "If we can only get to them during the first few weeks they are here, we can save a lot of suffering," Mrs. Standingbear feels.

Occasionally the Center makes demands on some of the municipal agencies; several months ago a committee headed by Mrs. Regina Johnson persuaded the Health Department to close and condemn a group of dwellings to which Indian arrivals were being referred by the Relocation Center. She had found the place while calling on a list of recent arrivals to invite them to a party at the Indian Center.

"You don't need to see them. They don't need to go to no parties." The landlady had tried to block her way. "They have all the parties they want right here."

In a sense, she was right. Mrs. Johnson found the shanties where they were staying crammed with mops and floor wax, thanks to the . . . "parties" given by neighboring women to which the Indians had been threateningly invited and instructed to "buy or else." But the parties were the least of the troubles of the twenty families unfortunate enough to land at the Government-approved address. The original building was in fair shape, but not the twenty flimsy "coops" built around it by the enterprising owner. Rent for the two-room shacks ranged between sixty and eighty dollars a month. Conveniences were minimal. The outdoor toilets were not functioning and the occupants of all twenty "apartments" had to depend upon the hospitality of one woman in the main building who had plumbing in working order and who was willing to permit them to use it. Bad cases of impetigo bred by filth afflicted most of the children, and young and old were generally suffering colds and bronchial disorders.

Why didn't they move? According to one young woman, the landlady announced that "anyone who made any trouble would be handed over to the police." . . .

The dedication of the staff and the volunteers has enabled the Center to perform almost incredible tasks. To a large degree, it has permitted the successful integration of hundreds of Indians, and it has minimized the problem of relocation in Los Angeles. Many cities have fared worse. In Minneapolis, Indians, who comprise less than 1 per cent of the city's general population, make up more than 10 per cent of the inmates at the men's workhouse and almost 70 per cent at the women's workhouse. Judge Luther Sletten of that city's municipal court calls it "one of our gravest social problems."

Obviously, something must be done with Indian lands inadequate to support the present and fast-growing population. One solution would be a kind of domestic Point Four program which would enable the Indians to make the most of the rich potential of reservation lands. [See "Proposed New Program of Congress," in Section VI, below.] Instead of being hindered, they should be encouraged to start businesses on reservations and in their communities. Young men with trade and technical training have had to leave home in order to utilize their newly acquired skills. One of the recent applicants for help in finding a job at the Los Angeles Indian Center was a former GI who had attended a barbers' school after his discharge. He returned to his reservation with an enthusiastic plan to open a barber shop, but government agents said no. Schools and extension classes should be instituted to help the Indians exploit their resources. If necessary, tribal funds which have been impounded could pay the costs of running them.

If, however, the program to dislodge the Indians is to be an all-out one, some educational program might be established to prevent the creation of another acute minority problem. It is imperative to slow down the relocation until the Indians have been prepared for integration.

The first step would be to institute a comprehensive orientation program in the relocation centers and on the reservations, providing some education and vocational training for the Indians who are to be sent into a mechanized urban environment.

Secondly, there should be a thorough screening process to make sure that those who are participating in the program are able to make the adjustment physically and mentally. Obviously, a knowledge of the English language is a prerequisite. So is at least fair health. Many of the new arrivals have been women in advanced pregnancy; many have been men with tuberculosis scars and other defects which make them unacceptable to industries.

Instead of being given the rosy picture of the promised land, the Indians who are leaving the security of their old life should have a more realistic picture of what lies before them. Most of them, Mrs. Standingbear says, are "woefully prepared." Few bring changes of clothing, bedding, or even cooking utensils—apparently under the delusion that the centers will "take care of everything."

Courses in household management are a must for women who have never seen electric lights and know nothing about shopping and little about cooking anything but the foods they have always eaten, which are rarely available. One woman was severely burned when her little tot tried to light the unfamiliar gas stove in their city dwelling.

A health insurance program is a must since the limited budgets of unskilled workers settling down in new environment rarely stretch to cover medical and hospital bills. And the municipalities charged with their integration should make exceptions to residence requirements in order to permit the new arrivals to avail themselves of necessary services. The American Indians, that long-suffering and inarticulate minority, have a great contribution to make to our culture. Unless they are permitted to do that, they will become a social and economic burden of magnitude—a shadow on the national conscience.

A SURVEY OF THE PROGRAM [6]

The Bureau of Indian Affairs has since 1952 conducted a controversial operation called the Voluntary Relocation Program. . . . By July 1, 1956, 12,625 reser-

[6] From "The American Indian Relocation Program," a report by La Verne Madigan, executive director, Association on American Indian Affairs, on the findings of a Relocation Survey team headed by Dr. Mary H. S. Hayes of the Association staff. The Association. 48 East 86th Street. New York 22. December 1956. p 1-22. Reprinted by permission.

vation Indians had already gone to cities under it and another 10,000 were expected to go by July 1, 1957.

The Association on American Indian Affairs . . . received from the Field Foundation a grant which made possible a survey of the actual operation of the Relocation Program on reservations and in cities. The Association stated publicly that it was beginning the survey without preconceptions and, on the strength of that assurance, received expected cooperation from Indian tribes, organizations and individuals and unexpectedly full cooperation from the Bureau of Indian Affairs. The Commissioner of Indian Affairs instructed Bureau personnel to turn over to Association investigators all statistical data requested, to allow free access to case files, and to answer all questions asked; these instructions were carried out. The survey was made in an atmosphere of such general frankness and eagerness to come at the truth that some of the soundest arguments in favor of the program were made by Indians and some of the most constructive criticisms of its shortcomings came from Indian Bureau personnel. . . .

The purpose of the Relocation Program is to seek and develop areas of opportunities where Indians may relocate and become self-supporting; disseminate information about such opportunities; assist Indians and their families, who voluntarily desire to do so, to move from the reservation, where opportunities for self-support are inadequate, to the new areas of their choice; provide or arrange for services to them in adjusting to the new environment; and aid them in securing permanent employment.

The challenge, according to the *Relocation Handbook*, which was compiled by the working personnel of the Bureau's Relocation Division, "is to show to the

Indian people that there is a better life awaiting them if they have the courage to request relocation." . . .

The Relocation branch of the Bureau of Indian Affairs according to our observations, is staffed by humane, singularly unbureaucratic people, dedicated, for better or for worse, to accomplishing many and successful relocations. . . . Some feel that public criticism aimed at the Congress and higher echelons of the Bureau for national Indian policy have landed on them, because what they do is all that is accomplished these days in Indian affairs. These are bitterly resentful, past the point of objectivity, of recent articles in *Harper's* and *Atlantic Monthly* which declare that the Relocation Program and, by inference, they are villainous. [See "Raid on the Reservations," in Section II, above, and "Uprooting the Indians," in this section, above.]

The Relocation Officers on the reservations are, for the most part, Indians or Westerners from Indian states, all meeting Civil Service requirements. The Indians qualify for the work by being Indian and by education. The non-Indians qualify by education and experience in the War Relocation Authority, which helped displaced Japanese-Americans during World War II, social agencies, labor unions or other branches of the Indian Service. Those interviewed in the course of this survey understand Indians and people. . . .

The Relocation Officers in the cities are, for the most part, non-Indian, although more Indians are being employed under the current budget to work as family counselors. These non-Indians have had experience in the War Relocation Authority, social agencies, and other branches of the Government which try to solve human problems. . . . They have to be city people in order to accomplish the work they must do, but they have much to learn about Indians from the trips to reservations which are scheduled for them. Unlike some critics of the program, they believe they can learn to understand an Indian's cultural values and that an Indian can learn, and even come to like theirs. They do not quarrel with an Indian's right to be Indian and culturally different in a reservation community. . . .

Almost without exception, the reservation offices appear to be manned by people who give all they have and have much to give. . . .

Reservation Indians know about the existence of the Relocation Program from speeches made at tribal council meetings; from little mimeographed folders on the counter at the trader's store, inviting anyone who is interested in year-round employment in a distant city to visit the Bureau office; from letters written home by others who went to the cities under the Program. In 1952 and 1953 they used to learn about it from Relocation Officers who went out on the reservation to recruit as for the Army. Such recruiting is still done in Oklahoma, where the Program is well regarded by Indians, and where Relocation is seen as opportunity. Relocation Officers in other areas do not usually do this now, partly because Indians are seeking relocation on their own initiative, and partly because public criticism of the quota-system used in the Program convinced the Bureau that the American people will tolerate the Program only to the extent that it is voluntary. . . .

The Relocation officer . . . in some cases tells [the Indian] that if he returns to the reservation he will be wiser, more skilled and in nobody's eyes a failure. The *Manual* does not say that a Relocation Officer may tell a man these things, . . . but they are said, as the man and his family receive their one-way tickets. . . .

The kindly service continues for a little while after the Indian family reaches the city. The man when he arrives at the railroad station has in his pocket an instruction sheet. It tells him to check his baggage, where it may be picked up later by a Relocation Office employee; and advises him, this once, to take a taxi to the Relocation Office. He has been told that he may turn to representatives of the Travelers Aid Society if some unforeseen confusion arises at the station, and he could not be told a better thing. . . .

The man and his family present themselves at the Relocation Office. . . . A receptionist, usually Indian, is expecting them. . . . The Relocation Officer, a woman in most cases where there is guidance work to be done, tells the man how to use the checking account in which his subsistence money will be deposited, and how to operate a dial telephone. She gives him a map of the city and tells him how to use it, although he is tired now and will probably forget what she said. She looks over her check-list of things to be remembered, and asks him whether he owns an alarm clock, promises to see that one is bought if he does not, and slips in a word of advice about getting to work on time. She tells him to rest with his family for the remainder of the day and to return to the office tomorrow in order that the Relocation Officer in charge of employment may refer him to a job. Then she takes the family to a cheap apartment house or hotel which is used to quarter large families until the man is working and permanent housing can be found near his place of employment. . . .

Housing, the need of which bedevils the entire country, is the score on which the Relocation Program has been most heavily attacked in the communities to which Indians are going in great numbers. It is the problem which Relocation Officers have been least successful in solving. . . .

By and large, the angriest criticism of Relocation housing is white, not Indian. The relocated Indians ought to criticize. They ought to want better, demand it, and get it, whether by their own effort or the Bureau's. However, there is Indian resignation to the third-best, and it is a sad indictment of the way in which our country has stunted the dreams of this group of its citizens. On the reservation, the man planning Relocation saw pictures of a refrigerator and a television set and heard about the flush toilet. In the city, no matter how shoddy his dwelling, he finds these. On this head he does not feel altogether betrayed. . . .

It has been said by some observers that relocating Indians are not being properly oriented for urban life. To others this comment seems to beg the question; to these it seems more appropriate to say that Indians are not being properly oriented for life anywhere in prosperous America, whether on reservations or in the cities, and that only the economic development of Indian areas will produce a generation of Indians who will expect and refuse to do without the best. This dilemma can never be unhorned by an orientation course geared solely and directly to the Relocation Program. . . .

The day after a man's arrival, or the same afternoon if he is not too tired, and his family feels safe in its temporary quarters, he goes to the Relocation Office for referral to a job. He is interviewed by an employment specialist who discusses his aptitudes and desires. . . . It is not difficult, in any event, to place him at the prevailing wage in a given industry, since city Relocation Offices are situated where employment is diversified and plentiful. . . . Wages are commensurate with those paid non-Indians for the same work; what is not commensurate, . . . is the size of the family to be supported on the wage.

The city Relocation Offices are usually able to place a man after from one to three referrals. . . The man's ability to adapt himself to and improve his skill in urban employment cannot be predicted before he tries. Whether he should be discouraged from trying at all because he may fail, or whether all Indians should be encouraged to remain in their reservation areas for the years it will take to produce a skilled generation is a question. . . .

While a man is seeking employment, the Relocation staff is performing various services for his family. One member helps hunt the permanent housing referred to above. Another . . . visits the home at least three times to take the mother out to buy clothes with the family's clothing allowance, to help her select used furniture for the $250 permitted for that, to enroll her at the prenatal clinic, to see that the children are registered in school, to learn whether the family is in any kind of trouble it has kept to itself. . . .

In general, unless a family seeks help of some kind after it has been relocated for a year, it gets none. The Relocation Program is carried out, avowedly, on the theory that a family succeeds or fails in the first six months to a year, and that after that time the family is on its own. Relocation Officers say that most Indians do not come to them for help after the first year because they do not need it; local critics of the program say that they do not come because they would not get it, that they will not go to community agencies for help because that is not their way, and that they go for help to other relocated Indians who may be worse off than they are. Neither the Bureau nor its critics can prove what they say, and no one really knows what happens to the majority of those Indians who do not return to the reservations after the year is up. . . .

City Relocation Offices have been instructed to interpret Indians to the community, to make full use of community resources. Generally, they have used the Travelers Aid Society under the Bureau's national agreement with that organization, have maintained nominal relations with the state employment services, and only token connections with mayors' committees on inmigrants and the fundamental organizations of the community. Public and private welfare agencies have been called upon in emergencies, but there has been failure to involve them in the planning of relocations and the responsibility for their success.

Some of the fundamental organizations of the community—clubs, churches, Indian centers—have rightly questioned the motives underlying the Relocation Program. They have, also rightly, exposed failures of operation in it. By concerning themselves almost exclusively with Federal Indian policy, however, and by failing at the same time to strengthen Indian newcomers' belief in their ability to succeed they have abdicated a responsibility and an opportunity. They have said, by their lack of action, exactly what the Bureau says by its lack of action in this field: that only the Bureau of Indian Affairs can understand or help American Indians. . . .

In Relocation cities, at the start, Indian centers developed as the avenue through which it was hoped the newcomers would enter the community. . . . Presently, as the Relocation Program swelled, national Indian interest organizations began to speak out about the program's motives and operations, and the local Indian centers joined the chorus. The top ranks of the Bureau of Indian Affairs and the national Indian interest organizations were used to this rough-and-tumble over Federal policy, and, as always, kept avenues of com-

munication open. The local Relocation Offices and the
city Indian centers, however, found that they were no
longer on speaking terms.

Today local personalities and egos are so deeply
involved in these feuds that one almost despairs of their
ever being able to work together for the benefit of relocated Indians. Almost, but not quite. In both cities
there are sincere people in the enemy camps, although
hardly anyone in either camp will admit that; and, involved in the affairs of both Indian centers, is the American Friends Service Committee, which can surely be
depended upon sooner or later to find the elusive passage-
way to peaceful cooperation. . . .

Relocated Indians arrive at their destinations on one-
way tickets, having signed a statement that they plan
to make a permanent home away from the reservation.
As pointed out earlier, many relocating Indians are told,
the signed statement notwithstanding, that they are not
to regard themselves as failures if they do not succeed
in the city. The Bureau says, quite freely, that of the
many Indians who return to reservations, some will go
back to the cities on their own and some will find better
local employment near home because of their city experience. The tribal councils which endorse the program
unreservedly—the Navahos and San Carlos Apaches,
for example—state cheerfully that this is the case.
They say that they expect most of their relocated people
to return in time to share in the big economic development which is being planned for their area. Certainly, no
serious effort is exerted on the reservations to convince
relocating Indians they may never return. . . .

To be objective, it is necessary to say these two
things. The Relocation Program, in and of itself, exerts
pressure of the benevolent type. The Relocation Program is being carried out in an Indian situation in which

huge pressures of the malign type are being exerted upon the Indian people.

The pressure exerted by the Relocation Program is the pressure of the goodness of the program itself. The program compels the interest of the reservation Indians not at gunpoint, but because it is warm-heartedly staffed and affords unprecedently generous financial help to people who want to try their luck in the world. . . .

The Bureau of Indian Affairs should make certain administrative changes which would bring the regulations governing the Relocation Program further into line with the spirit in which it is operated. These changes have to do with redefinition of the purpose of the Program, its extension to include resettlement in states where reservations are situated, and the provision, under certain circumstances, of return fare for relocated families. . . .

Congress should repeal House Concurrent Resolution 108 of the Eighty-third Congress, which declares it to be its intention to terminate the Indian tribes as rapidly as possible. . . .

The Bureau of Indian Affairs should urge the enactment of the American Indian Point Four Program by the Congress. [See "Proposed New Program of Congress," in Section VI, below.] The Bureau should, no longer taking shelter under the discredited mandate contained in House Concurrent Resolution 108, reverse its land policies as follows: it should say that it favors the continued trust protection of Indian land; it should declare a moratorium on Indian land sales and help the tribes purchase allotments which individual Indians want to sell; it should explicitly report, without resenting being asked to demonstrate its good faith to the Indian people, upon the progress of the announced plans for the economic development of Indian reservation communities. . . .

The American people in the large cities, seeing Indians living as strangers among them, must stop evading their share of the national responsibility by saying that the Bureau of Indian Affairs should take the Indians back to areas adjacent to the reservations where they will be happy; they must help them be happy where they are. The American people in the areas adjacent to Indian reservations, seeing Indians living in squalor among them, must stop insisting that the Bureau of Indian Affairs extend reservation service and status to Indians who have left their ethnic community for the mixed community just over the reservation border. They must accept the Indian's right to be there, or anywhere he wishes, and help him solve his problems in their own community's framework.

If Congress, the Bureau of Indian Affairs and the American people do these things—and all, not one must do them—the Relocation Program will be able to fulfill its promise and be what it should be: a minute part of a broad effort to open up America to the American Indians. As long as the Program remains the only program being carried out visibly and vigorously for the Indians, as long as the Indians have no economic choice between Relocation and something else, that long will the Program have to carry the blame for all of the Bureau's and the country's omissions.

VI. SUGGESTED PROGRAMS

EDITOR'S INTRODUCTION

This final section is concerned with proposals or programs offered by both Indian and non-Indian groups for long-range solution of the Indians' problems. The section opens with a plea by an Indian anthropologist that a full role be accorded to the Indians in working out their own salvation.

The "real issues" are explained by the president of the Inter-Tribal Council in Arizona. A resolution adopted by the National Congress of American Indians in 1954 offers a nine-point program, and a 1956 resolution of the same group sets forth seven specific tenets to guide Federal policy.

The American Friends Service Committee and National Council of Churches of Christ in United States of America both contribute blueprints for policy and administration. The section concludes with the text of a resolution for a "Point Four Program," introduced by Senator James E. Murray of Montana in behalf of the leading groups interested in Indian affairs.

HOW TO HELP INDIANS HELP THEMSELVES [1]

Speaking generally, segregation is thought of as a form of isolation of a particular class of persons, such as the foreign-born, or an ethnic group such as the Negroes, under conditions in which neither the group

[1] From "The Indian in American Society," by D'Arcy McNickle, member of the Flathead tribe of Montana, director of the American Indian Development Foundation, and former official of the United States Bureau of Indian Affairs. In *Social Welfare Forum, 1955* [proceedings of the forum of the National Conference of Social Work]. Columbia University Press. New York. 1955. p68-77. Reprinted by permission.

nor the individual has freedom of choice. The isolation
may be brought about by social custom and may be
enforced by legal sanctions. Desegregation of such a
group, its integration into the general population, involves a major process of education, in the case of social
custom; or legislative and judicial action, in the case of
legally sanctioned isolation. . . .

The isolation in which the Indians of the United
States live is not of this character. Indians may move
freely in and out of the society in which they habitually
live. They are subject to segregating factors, but no
more so than other members of the population might
be in similar circumstances: lack of education, lack of
trade skills, language barriers; and other cultural in-
hibitions. These conditioning factors apply to the individual, without destroying the basic freedom of the
group to move outward from their isolation.

In order to understand why Indian communities remain isolated from the mainstream, we must remember
that as white settlement spread to the interior, the Indian societies were like people caught in a flooding val-
ley, moving to higher ground as the invading waters
encroached upon them, until in time they were completely surrounded. Segregation was an act of self-
preservation, the motivation being a desire to keep what
they had. This motivation persists. We may consider it
unreasonable and self-limiting, but it is questionable
whether human action is ever entirely rational and logical. Nor is it likely that human conduct can be changed
merely by pointing out its irrationalities.

It is of interest to turn to the findings of a group
of social scientists who met in conference at the University of Chicago on February 20, 1954, to discuss a
series of assumptions current in Indian affairs in recent
years. The most basic of these assumptions reported to

the conference by John Provinse, former Assistant Co
missioner of Indian Affairs, was "the idea that assimi
tion of the American Indian into the normal stream ‿‿
American life is inevitable, that Indian tribes and communities will disappear."

The conference concluded:

> There was complete agreement on the part of the dis-
> cussants that this prediction is unwarranted. Most Indian
> groups in the United States, after more than one hundred
> years of Euro-American contact and in spite of strong
> external pressures, both direct and fortuitous, have not yet
> become assimilated in the sense of a loss of community
> identity and the full acceptance of American habits of thought
> and conduct. Nor can one expect such group assimilation
> within any short, predictable time period, say, one to four
> generations. The urge to retain tribal identity is strong, and
> operates powerfully for many Indian groups.

The group further concluded that while individual
Indians would doubtless make personal adjustments
which would enable them to become incorporated in the
general society,

> Despite external pressures, and internal change, most of
> the present identifiable Indian groups residing on reservations
> (areas long known to them as homelands) will continue
> indefinitely as distinct social units, preserving their basic
> values, personality, and Indian way of life, while making
> continual adjustments, often superficial in nature, to the
> economic and political demands of the larger society. [For
> further excerpts from the conference report, see "Outlook
> for the Indians," in Section II, above.—Ed.]

To admit that Indians live apart of their own choice
is not to agree that this is a good thing and that nothing
should be done to attempt to change it. The question
rather is to decide what kinds of change are desirable
and how to bring them about. . . .

First of all, the reservations generally have inadequate resources to provide a livelihood for the dependent population. However, these resources can be developed to a much greater extent, and thus a larger percentage of the residents could be supplied with livelihood. There are probably even a few reservations where the entire present population could enjoy a decent minimum living standard. Since these are the exceptions, however, Indians must look beyond the reservation, often to industrial urban areas, in order to find a livelihood and an expanding opportunity for their children.

In the second place, no society is static. The elders in an Indian group may exert their full force to prevent change in custom and belief, yet change will come. The masters in leadership, in whatever society, are the men who manage to make the compromise necessary to accept and adapt change without losing their following.

Even if there were no intervention to bring about desirable change, the forces which are acting upon Indian societies, as upon others, will result in drifts or trends in habits and values. Over a long enough period, Indian societies will be modified, for better or for worse. Can the process be guided? Can it be accelerated?

It is quite possible that affirmative answers can be given in both instances. But this will involve the adoption of administrative methods not now in vogue in Indian affairs.

It is believed, first of all, that if certain minimum needs of the Indian people are met, and if a climate of free choice is maintained, they will move away from isolation. The need for separate identification will diminish as Indians succeed in finding a place for themselves in the larger society.

The basic needs of the Indian people, in their present circumstances are these:

1. Health care, including training in sanitation and preventive health habits, to insure that the Indian population will not be an economic liability.

2. General education and vocational training to develop earning capacity.

3. Knowledge of the citizenship process to enable them to understand how to participate in local and national affairs.

Achievement of even these minimum objectives will require a readiness on the part of the Indian people to adopt them as their own. To create this readiness is a problem in method—a problem which administrators of Indian affairs have not solved. . . .

The administration of Indian affairs in recent years has avoided the more obvious aspects of coercion, yet it still fails to involve the participation of the people whose affairs are being administered.

The recommendation of the Meriam survey team [in 1928] that the Indian Service be organized as an educational effort was never carried out. . . .

In still another aspect, administration is self-defeating. Because programs are designed to provide services rather than to train people, it becomes essential that the programs be staffed by technically trained people capable of accomplishing the goals set by the Administration and by Congress. The personnel of the Bureau of Indian Affairs has in recent years become a highly competent professional staff. Yet the farther it has advanced in developing professional competence the farther it has removed itself from the people it serves. . . .

Before integration of a people in a larger society can take place, a process of acculturation must be set in motion. But the acculturation process is not a physical conquest; it resists pressures applied from the outside. It is not a one-way process of adding new ideas or ways of behaving to patterns that already exist. It is essentially a creative process in which there is selection, rejection, and modification or adaptation of elements. When cultures come into contact, one may not predict what will be accepted and what rejected, and it is by no means certain that only the desirable elements of the offering culture will be accepted. The elements accepted are likely to be in some way identifiable with those already imbedded in the receiving culture. . . .

Acculturation as a process starts with individuals. This is the clue which administrators have failed to discover. The basis of administrative action has been one of exterior application of policy and program. Thus at times there has been an almost complete reliance on legislation to bring about social change. When a law failed to achieve its purpose, the administrator looked to a failure in the law rather than in the principle of action involved, and requested amendments to the law. . . .

Unfortunately, administrators and congressmen have not yet given up the notion that solutions can be found in legislative action. . . .

It is the individual and the internal structure of a group to which we must look if we expect to bring about the integration of the Indian people in the general society of the United States. This will involve seeking out in each Indian group individuals who, while they have respected status in the group, have a predilection for some of the well-being which lies beyond their grasp. This implies an individual who is probably bilingual, who may have some formal schooling and who has probably traveled and worked on the "outside." Such schooling and such work experience as he has had, however, have not been sufficient to turn him away from his people or to awaken in the minds of his relatives and peers the suspicion that he seeks to rise above them.

Individuals answering this generalized description are to be found in practically every Indian group. Often they are held in small esteem by their white neighbors and by the very administrators who struggle with a task they cannot master. The fact that they have been exposed to outside society, yet choose to remain with their own people, is enough to stigmatize them for having "returned to the blanket."

Up to a certain point, these individuals usually live an aimless life on the reservation. If they had received enough schooling and picked up enough experience, that might have carried them beyond old boundary lines. However, what they received did not help them to achieve a satisfactory adjustment to the new environment, so they returned home. The process of going and coming repeats itself many times, but eventually they attain the age to which respect and authority are attached. They begin to function in the native community in a way that was never possible on the outside. Aimlessness then gives way to purpose. They become the men who make up the tribal councils and the livestock associations on the reservations. Often they are the men who say "no" to Government programs and find themselves in the bad graces of administrative personnel.

Yet these individuals may be the very instruments through whom policy and program can be carried out. Since they do have status and are respected in their communities, they are in a position to urge the acceptance of change and to promote ideas from the outside.

Generally, this native leadership will need training, the extent and kind of which will vary according to the needs of the community and the skills and experience of the leaders to be incorporated in the program. The training in most cases would be nontechnical in nature and relatively inexpensive to provide. The leaders would not be expected to carry the technical aspects of a program, but would be used as sponsors of programs and as liaison between the community and the technical program.

Behind these community leaders, forming a second line of action, would be placed technically trained personnel, some of whom might also be members of the community. This second group need not speak the native language, though it would be important that members of this group have some knowledge of the history and culture of the community. At least this technical group should know enough about the community to be able to follow the directions of, and to work at the tempo suggested by, the community workers. The folly of employing skilled personnel in situations where their services are not understood and their instructions cannot be followed would be avoided if they could rely upon, and work through, a corps of trained community workers.

The objective of any program should not end with the completion of a task or the contribution of a service. The objective rather should be the process established for task and service performance. To benefit the people involved in a situation it is of paramount importance that they learn how to organize and carry out community programs. It is of lesser long-range importance that a school be built or a road completed, even though there is an immediate benefit in such achievements. Our concern should be with the growth of a people, and growth does not occur, except vegetable-wise, where there is no learning experience.

AN INDIAN SPEAKS OUT [2]

American citizens, including public officials, generally don't know what the Indian issues really are. The issues are not assimilation, or integration, or emancipation, or Government control over the Indian person, or civil rights in the usual sense of the words.

The real issues are continuing ownership of land; development of human and natural resources; protection of rights solemnly promised by treaty and law; honor in Government dealing with conquered peoples; our day in court on our claims; real opportunity for education of the same quality as is available to non-Indian citizens; adequate Federal assistance in reservation development toward the end our communities may thrive and contribute to the [general] prosperity . . . ; an end to bureaucratic dictatorship and unnecessary Federal regulations; an end to wasteful and constantly changing, insensitive administration of our affairs in favor of a constant policy of minimum interference and maximum assistance to us to help ourselves.

There is something radically wrong with the kind of Federal supervision of Indian affairs we have had when after 135 years of Indian administration, Indians face more problems than ever. . . .

What are some of the things that are wrong? Some of the things that could be done to help? Indian tribes in this country today need long-term loans and grants for resources development, both natural resources and human resources. They need a minimum of regulation and control and a maximum of encouragement and technical assistance. Indian tribes need the kind of program that

[2] From "Wesley Explains Real Indian Issues," by Clarence Wesley, president, Inter-Tribal Council. National Congress of American Indians. 1346 Connecticut Avenue. Washington 6, D.C. 1 p. 1956. (Originally published in *Arizona Republic*, June 23, 1956, and included in extension of remarks of Senator Barry M. Goldwater, Republican, Arizona, in *Congressional Record*, June 26, 1956.) Reprinted by permission.

this nation is making possible in underdeveloped countries in other parts of the world. [See "Proposed New Program of Congress," in this section, below.]

As to Federal appropriations for Indian affairs: True, the United States Congress has appropriated millions of dollars to the Bureau of Indian Affairs and does so each year. Beyond that fact, several questions need to be raised. (1) Indians don't receive any payments from the Government, or any services that other citizens don't receive out of tax moneys, from the same source. Indians don't get payments from the Federal Government just because they are Indians.

(2) How much of the Federal appropriation for Indian affairs actually benefits Indians? Many of us who work and plead for development of our resources contend that most of this appropriation goes into salaries— in the central office in Washington, D.C., in eight area offices over the Indian country, and in many reservation field offices. All of them have huge staffs compared to anything that Indian tribes or Indian organizations have to work with. Indian tribes and leaders have protested bitterly against the operations of the area offices on the grounds they furnish just another layer of bureaucrats, they form another buckpassing stop, they duplicate services.

The general attitude of tribal officials and Indian leaders is that authority and responsibility should be vested in the local reservation superintendent where it used to be. Problems of tribes vary widely, and if the reservation superintendent is a good man and tries to work with the Indians, he can do more good than all the higher brass put together. A good superintendent and the tribe's governing officials working together can accomplish wonders and bring about changes of lasting and permanent value on a reservation.

(3) Very few people realize that many tribes pay many of their own tribal employees and administration costs—in other words, many tribes pay much of their own way out of their own tribal income. . . .

Money and political power are needed to protect what little is left of our once great natural resources and to develop them not only for our own improved conditions, but for the general prosperity of our state. Modern tribal business corporations, healthy, prosperous, wholesome communities are our goal. . . .

Since the courts settled the matter of allowing us to vote only in 1948, our people need much information and encouragement to exercise this effective tool in our behalf. Our congressmen in Washington are showing more respect for our wishes and our needs as we become more active in our voting citizenship.

INDIAN CONGRESS PRESENTS VIEWPOINT [3]

Whereas, the Government of the United States has the primary responsibility for the ultimate adjustment of the affairs of the Indian people, a responsibility vested in the National Government by provisions of the Federal Constitution and made specific in numerous treaties, agreements, acts of Congress, and regulatory measures; and

Whereas, in its efforts to carry out its responsibility in this field the United States has depended too exclusively on law and regulation as the means of dealing with complex human problems, and at times has even resorted to the exercise of its full legal

[3] From "Resolutions Passed by 13th Annual Convention, National Congress of American Indians, at Salt Lake City, Utah, September 24-28, 1956. Mimeographed. The Congress. 1346 Connecticut Avenue. Washington 6, D.C. 1956. p 1-17. Reprinted by permission.

authority to enforce decisions which later proved to be erroneous and harmful to the interests of the Indian people; and

Whereas, it is our firm belief that many decisions affecting Indian welfare can only effectively be made by the people whose lives and property are at stake and not by individuals in positions of authority, however well trained in special fields such individuals may be; and

Whereas, we are well aware of the earnest desire of the Congress of the United States and of the Executive Branch of the Government to bring about the honorable discharge of the responsibilities and obligations assumed by the United States, and we, speaking for Indian tribes and many individual Indians of the United States and Alaska, having a desire to promote the ultimate adjustment of Indian life ways within the larger American community in a manner to preserve Indian cultural values; and

Whereas, the declaration of national policy stated in House Concurrent Resolution 108 (Eighty-third Congress) is a flagrant example of an attempt to solve complex social, economic, cultural and legal problems by merely legalistic means;

Now, therefore, we urge the immediate repeal of House Concurrent Resolution 108 . . . and the substitution therefor of the following as a statement of national policy and as a guide to administrative action:

A plan of development be prepared for each reservation, pueblo, colony, village or other designation by which Indians of the United States and Alaska are recognized and under which designation lands or other assets are held in trust, whether such lands or assets are fully defined or not, such plans to be designed to bring about maximum utilization of physical resources by the dependent population and the development of that population to its full potential, such plans to be prepared by the Indians of the respective groups, with authority to call upon agencies of the Federal Government for technical assistance, and the ultimate purpose of such planning to be the growth and development of the resources of the people rather than the heedless termination of Federal responsibility for such people;

That requests for annual appropriations of funds be based on the requirements for carrying into effect these individual development plans, and the annual operating budget for the Bureau of Indian Affairs, to include sufficient funds to carry out the program needs of each planning group;

That such annual budgets include adequate funds to provide for the credit needs and for capital investment required for the full development of Indian resources;

That determinations with respect to the disposition of property or any actions which may affect treaty rights or agreements be based on agreement between an Indian tribe or group and the United States;

That any transfer of services now provided by the United States for the benefit of Indians be jointly planned with the Indians; and

That Public Law 280 (Eighty-third Congress) be modified to provide that the assumption by states of jurisdiction in criminal and civil actions in Indian reservations be brought about only after negotiation between a state and an Indian tribe and only to the extent from time to time agreed upon by the Indian tribe;

That the Indian groups be kept fully advised at all stages of pending legislation in which their interests may be involved and that the Secretary of the Interior likewise keep them advised of regulatory measures which may be

proposed for adoption, and accord full opportunity to the
Indian groups and their representatives to be heard and
have their needs and views considered in the formulation,
modification or repeal of regulatory measures.

PROPOSALS FOR A 1957 PROGRAM [4]

A Legislative Program

1. One year ago . . . [the Association on American
Indian Affairs] expressed the hope that a bill would be
introduced in the Congress establishing a long-range
American Indian Point Four Program. Then Senator
Murray [Democrat, Montana] introduced an appropriate
resolution, but it was not enacted. Now Senator Murray
has introduced Senate Concurrent Resolution 3 . . . [see
"Proposed New Program of Congress," in this section,
below]. We hope that it will be passed by the Eighty-fifth
Congress.

2. Last year we also called for amendments to the
Depressed Areas bills to make specific provisions for aid
to Indians. One of the bills, S. 2663, was so amended
and passed the Senate in that form. It was, however, not
considered by the House.

We hope that S. 2663 will be reintroduced and passed.
However, as presently worded it provides that Federal
loans can be made in a depressed area only if some money
is put up locally. We believe that this will be impossible
on many Indian reservations and hope that the bill will
be further amended to permit the foregoing requirement
to be waived in the most destitute cases.

3. We have in the past supported bills to solve the
problem of heirship lands (Indian land in which two or

[4] From "A Legislative Program for American Indians" and "An Administrative Program for American Indians." *Indian Affairs.* no 19:4-6. January 1957. Reprinted by permission.

more heirs hold undivided interests. As the number of heirs continues to multiply, no effective ownership is exercised by any of them.) Bills to readjust Indian land holdings were introduced in the Eighty-fourth Congress. . . . We hope that they will be reintroduced and passed and that existing loan funds and/or additional Federal funds will be authorized to be used to carry the readjustment program into effect.

4. The threat of unwanted extension of state control, as authorized by Sections 6 and 7 of Public Law 280, Eighty-third Congress, still hangs over many Indian tribes. A bill to repeal those sections (S. 51) passed the Senate last year but failed in the House. We hope that it will be reintroduced and passed.

5. The Public Health Service has developed a program for the improvement of domestic water and sanitation facilities on Indian reservations. A bill to authorize this program to be carried into effect (H.R. 9150) was introduced last year. We hope that it will be reintroduced and passed in the Eighty-fifth Congress.

6. During the Eighty-fourth Congress hearings were held on H.R. 8484, a bill providing scholarships for deserving Indian students. We hope that the Eighty-fifth Congress will enact a scholarship program such as was provided by H.R. 8484.

An Administrative Program

The economic development of reservation areas should be the governing goal of the Bureau of Indian Affairs, and it should be accomplished by the following steps, among others:

1. The Bureau and the Department of the Interior should request outright repeal of House Concurrent Resolution 108 of the Eighty-third Congress on the ground

that the Bureau's plans for Indian economic development cannot be carried out under an outmoded congressional mandate calling for the rapid termination of Federal assistance and supervision.

2. The Bureau and the Department of the Interior should recommend that Congress authorize the American Indian Point Four Program . . . ; and, even prior to such congressional action, the Bureau should recast its own machinery, insofar as that is within its administrative power, in order that it may function immediately as an American Indian Point Four agency.

3. The Bureau should state publicly that its past land policies are not consonant with its present plans for Indian economic development, and that, pending the economic development of Indian areas, it no longer favors the removal of Indian land from trust status as rapidly as possible.

4. The Bureau should declare an immediate moratorium on sales of Indian land to non-Indians in order to stabilize the size of Indian communities, and should use the idle cash balance of $7,832,979.29 in the Revolving Credit Fund to assist tribes to purchase individual allotments which individual Indian owners desire to sell.

5. The Bureau should sponsor and promote land adjustment programs, including the purchase of additional lands when needed for Indian community development.

6. The Bureau, in evolving plans for the economic development of Indian areas, should request the cooperation in specific ways of Indian and Indian interest organizations, which have asked for such plans and have it in their power to further them.

7. As part of community development in Indian areas and in order to create a wage economy, the Bureau should abandon its present policy of making contracts for con-

struction, road and similar work to be done on reservations, and should employ Indians wherever possible. Similarly, professionally trained Indian employees of the Bureau should be recalled from posts distant from their home areas and stationed where their knowledge may be of service to their own communities.

8. The population figures used by the Bureau to measure the need for and numerical success of the Relocation Program should be used to measure the need for and success of economic development of Indian areas; and Relocation quotas and/or maxima should be adjusted annually and publicly in relation to the increased number of people reservations have been made able to support.

9. An economic alternative to relocation in industrial cities should be provided for the Indian people through the measures described immediately above, and the Relocation Program itself should be improved in the specific ways recommended in the Association's report. [See "A Survey of the Program," in Section V, above.] These improvements include redefinition of the program as a service to provide adult education, financial assistance to Indians to return to reservations under certain circumstances; extension of the Relocation Program's financial services to include Indians who find steady employment in their home states through their own state employment services; resettlement in cities smaller than Chicago and Los Angeles; increased participation in Relocation planning by elected tribal officials and by social agencies in the cities to which Indians are relocated; insurance that no Indian will be forced to relocate because he cannot obtain welfare assistance locally; stricter health examinations of families planning relocation; more intelligent use in the Relocation cities of the community resources upon which relocated Indians will have to depend when Relocation Program services are discontinued.

10. The United States Public Health Service has, at the request of Congress, prepared a report on Indian medical care and, pending its release, recommendations for improved service will be withheld. The Public Health Service should, however, reach an agreement with the Bureau of Indian Affairs on a definition of eligibility for medical care, in order that patients, still tribally enrolled and owning their own trust allotments, may not be turned away from Indian hospitals because they have been absent from the reservation for a few months. Since health education on reservations can play a decisive part in the success of a relocation to a large city, the United States Public Health Service should also take the initiative in offering cooperation to the Bureau's Relocation staff in devising orientation courses for Indians planning relocation.

THE FRIENDS GIVE THEIR VIEWS [5]

The American Friends Service Committee's Indian Program is one of many possible approaches to the problems that confront the Indians of the United States today. Other organizations and individuals have similar objectives which encourage Indian self-help.

But in the end, the success or failure of all programs in this field will depend on the willingness of the Indians, the Federal Government, and all others concerned to cooperate in setting positive goals and working toward them. So long as Federal policy arouses the fear and antagonism of a considerable number of Indians, little progress can be expected.

If the Federal Government would suspend what sometimes appears as legislative and administrative harassment

[5] From "The Spirit They Live In," pamphlet. American Friends Service Committee. 20 South 12th Street. Philadelphia 7. 1956. p 18-20. Reprinted by permission.

of the tribes, it might become a helpful partner in Indian-conceived programs of social action and resource development. If Government agencies responsible for administering Indian affairs were to become real advocates of Indian needs, they might be able to drastically reduce their staffs and expenditures as these needs are met.

More than anything else, Indians want to feel a renewed faith in the promises of their Government and its ability to carry them out. As citizens who are under-privileged and have been wronged they are entitled to sympathetic and understanding assistance.

Believing these goals are possible to attain, the American Friends Service Committee suggests the following five principles of action as steps toward a more humane and equitable Indian policy:

1. Americans should know their Indian fellow-citizens. Basic to the understanding of Indian needs and aspirations is an appreciation of their unique contributions to American culture. All Americans can learn much from each other, so long as their relations are founded on mutual respect and acceptance of cultural differences.

2. Indians should be free to choose a way of life. That this freedom of choice may be real, educational opportunities should be broadened to fit individuals for reservation or urban living. Adequate funds and technical assistance should be made available to individuals and tribal groups willing to develop reservation resources; help should be extended to those who wish to move from the Indian community.

3. Indian groups should be helped to plan for the future. When Indian communities ask for assistance, they should be helped to organize. They should have easy access to all information about their resources and should be made aware of services available to them. All com-

munity programs should be based on plans prepared by the people themselves.

4. Indian tribes should be free to manage their affairs. Self-government should be encouraged, as a logical step toward fuller participation in society. When and if an Indian group decides, by democratic process, that its interests would best be served by abandonment of its political or economic identity, it should be assisted in the orderly transfer of its functions.

5. Indians should not be hurried or forced into fuller participation in American society. Indians, like any people excluded from a broader culture, are often unconvinced about the benefits of Western civilization and may be extremely cautious in adopting modern ideas. They have seen the systematic destruction of their own civilization. They are suspicious and lack the background to appreciate the non-Indian's attempt to change them. All Americans must recognize the problem as their own creation. Non-Indians must, therefore, be willing to invest time, patience and open-mindedness until they "feel and understand their life and the spirit they live in."

CHURCH GROUP SUGGESTS PROCEDURES [6]

A primary objective of our democratic society is that Indian people along with all other American citizens shall have opportunities for self-development in family and religious life, in education, employment, and for participation in the benefits of housing, medical care, public services and accommodation. Indians can and should be helped to participate more fully in the benefits and responsibilities of the American community. We recognize that America has been enriched by the Indian cultural heritage and that the values thus brought into our society

[6] From "A Pronouncement on Indian Affairs, adopted March 3, 1955. Processed. National Council of the Churches of Christ in the United States of America, Division of Home Missions. 257 Fourth Ave. New York 10. 1955. p 1-4. Reprinted by permission.

should be conserved. We therefore affirm the necessity for assuring to each Indian tribe or band the right to preserve, to the extent consistent with the general welfare, its own cultural identity. In any actions terminating its special relationship to Indian tribes, we believe that the Federal Government has a responsibility to act in accordance with objectives stated in this paragraph. . . .

The National Council of Churches believes that the following specific considerations will contribute to the orderly transition of Indian tribes or bands from trusteeship status to full participation in community life.

1. Legislation to terminate trusteeship should protect the Indian tribe or band against unilateral Government abrogation of contracts or treaties which exist between the tribe or band and the Federal Government. Therefore provision should be included in such legislation for the renegotiation of such contractual agreements.

2. Legislation and the administrative procedure of Government agencies should provide for consultation and negotiation between Federal officials and representatives duly authorized by the Indian tribe or band. In this way the social and economic problems which confront the tribe or band during the transition period may be handled equitably. The tribe or band should have an opportunity to develop plans or a program for administering its own affairs either as a group or as individuals as the tribe or band itself may decide.

3. Negotiations should be carried on between the Bureau of Indian Affairs and other agencies of the Federal Government as well as with state and local governmental agencies to work out mutually acceptable arrangements. These should guarantee that the customary governmental services shall be fully available to Indians without segregation or discrimination. Federal services should not be terminated until such arrangements have been made.

4. Programs should be continued and greatly expanded:

For the development and use of reservation resources;

For a solution of the fractionated land problem in a way that protects the Indians' interests;

For the development of those social and economic skills that make possible normal adjustment to employment; and

For assisted voluntary relocation.

5. Greatly increased attention should be given to programs for fundamental education and health education. These programs should conserve the values of family life and be in harmony with accepted principles of education.

6. Programs of education for the entire community are necessary to develop an understanding of the changing status of Indian tribes or bands and its effect on Indian American families and individuals.

The National Council of Churches believes that the churches have a particular responsibility through their interdenominational and denominational agencies to contribute to a constructive process of change as Indians face new adjustments to the American community. Every step [should be] taken to prepare local congregations to understand the problems and to [promote] helpful relationships between Indians and others in the community.

PROPOSED NEW PROGRAM OF CONGRESS [7]

Whereas it is the understanding of Congress that its responsibility in the American Indian problem cannot be fulfilled by the dispersal of Indian communities, but by the continuous development of their human and economic potential; and

[7] Text of Senate Concurrent Resolution 3, 85th Congress, 1st session, a resolution relating to raising the standard of living of the American Indian, introduced by Senator James E. Murray (Democrat, Montana), January 3, 1957. p 1-3. Text supplied by courtesy of Senator Murray.

Whereas it is recognized that Indian communities cannot be considered to have reached the American level of well-being until the principles of consent of the governed, self-determination, and local self-government are operative, nor until Indian opportunities in economy, education, and health are measurably equal to those of their fellow citizens; and

Whereas the American "Point Four program," as it has been applied successfully in underdeveloped areas of the world, reveals tested techniques whereby American Indian communities may be so developed: Now, therefore, be it

Resolved by the Senate (the House of Representatives concurring), That the Bureau of Indian Affairs shall be, by definition, an agency to assist American Indian communities to reach the level of well-being enjoyed by other communities in the United States, and the governing program of the Bureau of Indian Affairs shall be an American Indian Point Four program.

It is declared to be the sense of Congress that this program shall be offered to the American Indian communities without exacting termination of Federal protection of Indian property or of any other Indian rights as its price; that Indian culture and identity shall not be restricted or destroyed; that technical guidance and financial assistance shall be made available; that the request for assistance shall come from the Indians themselves after each Indian group has studied itself in terms of its own needs; that an impartial effort shall be made to deal with the development of natural resources to maximum capacity, to develop the full capabilities of industrial and agricultural production, of improvements in housing, nutrition, clothing, sanitation, and health, and of the resettlement on their initiative of individuals and families in other areas; that technical assistance shall be given to long-term general, vocational, technical, and professional education to enable American Indians to share fully in our total American society and to contribute to it; and that older, revered values shall be respected and used as new forms of living are introduced.

It is further declared to be the sense of Congress that the Secretary of the Interior shall review all programs of the Bureau of Indian Affairs in order to develop its activities to further an American Indian Point Four program, and that he shall report to Congress at the earliest possible date his recommendations for such legislation as may be necessary to accomplish the purposes of this resolution.

Finally, it is declared to be the sense of Congress that Federal protection and services shall be ended for any tribe, band, or group only when such unit shall have adopted a plan for its organization and operation under state law, and such plan shall have been approved by the appropriate state and by the Secretary of the Interior prior to its submission to the Congress.

BIBLIOGRAPHY

An asterisk (*) preceding a reference indicates that the article or a part of it has been reprinted in this book.

BIBLIOGRAPHIES

Harvard Law Record. Bibliography on American Indian affairs. 7p. mimeo. The Record. 23 Everett St. Cambridge, Mass. '55.

Indian Rights Association. Suggested reading list. 3p. mimeo. The Association. 1505 Race St. Philadelphia 2. n.d.

Sondley Reference Library. American Indians. (Leaves from the Sondley. v2, no2) 12p. The Library. Asheville, N.C. '49.

BOOKS, PAMPHLETS, AND DOCUMENTS

*American Friends Service Committee. Spirit they live in. 19p. The Committee. 20 S. 12th St. Philadelphia 7. '56.

American Friends Service Committee. Indians of California, past and present. 36p. The Committee, 1830 Sutter St. San Francisco 15. '56.

*Association on American Indian Affairs. American Indian relocation program. 22p. The Association. 48 E. 86th St. New York 28. '56.

Association on American Indian Affairs. Menominee termination problems, 1955. William Zimmerman, Jr. 2p. processed. The Association. 48 E. 86th St. New York 28. '55.

*Association on American Indian Affairs. Statement on Indian land alienation, issued jointly with Indian Rights Association, Friends Committee on National Legislation, and National Congress of American Indians, June 27, 1955. 2p. mimeo. The Association. 48 East 86th St. New York 28. '55.

Carter, E. R. Gift is rich. 156p. Friendship Press. New York. '54.

Center for Information on America. How about the condition of the Indians? 4p. The Center. Washington, Conn. '53.

Cole, Stewart, and Cole, Mildred. Minorities and the American promise. 319p. Harper & Bros. New York. '55.

Cory, D. M. Within two worlds. 177p. Friendship Press. New York. '55.

Deloria, E. C. Speaking of Indians. 163p. Friendship Press. New York. '44.

Denver Art Museum. Department of Indian Art. Mistaken ideas about Indians. 4p. The Museum. 1300 Logan St. Denver 3, Colo. '51.

Dexter, E. F. Doors toward the sunrise. 116p. Friendship Press. New York. '55.

Embree, E. R. Indians of the Americas. 260p. Houghton Mifflin Co. Boston. '39.

Embry, Carlos. America's concentration camps. 242p. David McKay Co. New York. '56.

Encyclopaedia Britannica (consult Index volume under "Indians, North American").

Fletcher, S. E. American Indian. 152p. Grosset & Dunlap. New York. '54.

Foreman, Grant. Indian removal; the emigration of the five civilized tribes of Indians. new ed. 415p. University of Oklahoma Press. Norman. '53.

Hodge, F. W. ed. Handbook of American Indians north of Mexico. (United States Bureau of American Ethnology. Bulletin 30) 2v. Government Printing Office. Washington, D.C. '07-10.

Indian Rights Association. Why Indians need our help. 6p. The Association. 1505 Race St. Philadelphia 2, '52.

Institute of Ethnic Affairs. Crisis in United States Indian Affairs. 4p. The Institute. 617 Greenwich. Falls Church, Va. '52.

Institute of Ethnic Affairs. Indian Bureau reverts to obsolete policy of spoliation. 3p. The Institute. 617 Greenwich. Falls Church, Va. '50.

Institute of Ethnic Affairs. "Terminating" the American Indian; circular letter by John Collier, president, February 13, 1954. 5p. mimeo. The Institute. 617 Greenwich. Falls Church, Va. '54.

Kenton, Edna. Indians of North America. 2v. 579p. Harcourt, Brace & Co. New York. '27.

La Farge, Oliver. Changing Indian. 184p. University of Oklahoma Press. Norman. '42.

La Farge, Oliver. Pictorial history of the American Indian. 272p. Crown Publishers. New York. '56.

La Farge, Oliver. Record, 1949-50. 8p. Association on American Indian Affairs, 48 E. 86th St. New York 28. '50.

La Gorce, J. A. and Sterling, M. W. Indians of the Americas. National Geographic Society. Washington 6, D.C. '57.

Lindquist, G. E. E. Indian in American life. 180p. Friendship Press. New York. '44.

Loram, C. T. and McIlwraith, eds. North American Indian today. 361p. University of Toronto Press. Toronto, Canada. '43.

MacGregor, F. C. Twentieth century Indians. 127p. G. P. Putnam's Sons. New York. '41.

Marriott, Alice. Greener fields. 350p. Thomas Y. Crowell Co. New York. '53.
    Chapter 12. p 154-77.

McNickle, D'Arcy. They came here first. 325p. J. B. Lippincott Co. Philadelphia. '49.

McNicol, D. M. Amerindians. 341p. Frederick A. Stokes Co. New York. '37.

Meriam, Lewis, and others. Problem of Indian administration. 872p. Johns Hopkins Press. Baltimore. '28.

*National Conference of Social Work. Social welfare forum, 1955 [proceedings of the forum of the Conference]. 265p. Columbia University Press. New York. '55.
    Reprinted in this book: Indian in American society. D'Arcy McNickle. p68-77.

National Congress of American Indians. Address by Joseph R. Garry, president, at 13th annual convention, Salt Lake City, Utah, September 24-28, 1956. The Congress. 1346 Connecticut Ave. Washington 6, D.C. '56.

National Congress of American Indians. Point Four program for American Indians. 10p. processed. The Congress. 1346 Connecticut Ave. Washington 6, D.C. '54.

*National Congress of American Indians. Resolutions passed by 13th annual convention, Salt Lake City, Utah, September 24-28, 1956. 17p. processed. The Congress. 1346 Connecticut Ave. Washington 6, D.C. '56.

*National Congress of American Indians. Story of two congresses; address by Representative Lee Metcalf, Montana, before 13th annual convention, Salt Lake City, Utah, September 24-28, 1956. 7p. mimeo. The Congress. 1346 Connecticut Ave. Washington 6, D.C. '56.

*National Congress of American Indians. U.S. Government policy towards American Indians; a few basic facts; revised to October 1, 1956. 11p. mimeo. The Congress. 1346 Connecticut Ave. Washington 6, D.C. '56.

*National Congress of American Indians. Wesley explains real Indian issues. 1p. The Congress. 1346 Connecticut Avenue. Washington 6, D.C. '56.
    Originally published in Arizona Republic, June 23, 1956, and included in extension of remarks of Senator Barry M. Goldwater, Arizona, in Congressional Record, June 26, 1956.

*National Council of the Churches of Christ in the United States of America. Pronouncement on Indian affairs, adopted March 3, 1955. 4p. The Council. Division of Home Missions. 297 Fourth Ave. New York 10. '55.

Priest, L. B. Uncle Sam's stepchildren. 310p. Rutgers University Press. New Brunswick, N.J. '42.

Radin, Paul. Story of the American Indian. rev. ed. 391p. Liveright Publishing Corp. New York. '44.

Schmeckebier, L. F. Office of Indian Affairs. 591p. Johns Hopkins Press. Baltimore. '27.

Seymour, F. W. We called them Indians. 280p. Appleton. New York. '40.

*Shotwell, L. R. This is the American Indian. 33p. Friendship Press. New York. '55.

Trotter, G. A. From feather, blanket and tepee. 90p. Vantage Press. New York. '56.

Underhill, R. M. Red man's America. 400p. University of Chicago Press. Chicago. '53.

United States. Congress. 79th Congress, 2d session. An act to create an Indian Claims Commission, to provide for the powers, duties and functions thereof, and for other purposes. Public Law 726. Chapter 959. 8p. Indian Claims Commission. Washington 25, D.C. '46.

United States. Congress. 84th Congress, 2d session. An act to terminate the existence of the Indian Claims Commission and for other purposes. Public Law 767. Chapter 670. 1 p. Bureau of Indian Affairs. Washington 25, D.C. '56.

United States. Department of the Interior. Bureau of Indian Affairs. Address by G. L. Emmons, read at Triennial Conference of National Fellowship of Indian Workers, Estes Park, Colorado, July 11, 1955. 10p. processed. The Bureau. Washington 25, D.C. '56.

*United States. Department of the Interior. Bureau of Indian Affairs. Commissioner's memorandum of May 16, 1955, on issuance of patents in fee to competent applicants. 1 p. mimeo. The Bureau. Washington 25, D.C. '55.

United States. Department of the Interior. Bureau of Indian Affairs. Indian, our fellow citizen and brother. 2p. processed. Haskell Institute. Lawrence, Kans. '56.

United States. Department of the Interior. Bureau of Indian Affairs. Questions on Indian culture. (Pamphlet 1) 19p. Haskell Institute. Lawrence, Kans. '56.

United States. Department of the Interior. Bureau of Indian Affairs. Resident population on Indian reservations, 1950. 13p. The Bureau. Washington 25, D.C. '51.

United States. Department of the Interior. Bureau of Indian Affairs. Situation of American Indians in the United States. 5p. processed. Haskell Institute. Lawrence, Kans. n.d.

United States. Department of the Interior, Bureau of Indian Affairs. Summary of 1955 Indian legislation. 5p. processed. The Bureau. Washington 25, D.C. '56.

*United States. Department of the Interior. Bureau of Indian Affairs. Summary of 1953 legislation. 2p. processed. The Bureau. Washington 25, D.C. '54.

*United States. Department of the Interior. Bureau of Indian Affairs. Voluntary Relocation Program. 2p. processed. The Bureau. Washington 25, D.C. '56.

*United States. Senate. Senate Concurrent Resolution 3, relating to raising the standard of living of the American Indian, introduced by Senator James E. Murray, January 3, 1957. 85th Congress, 1st session.
    Same. Indian Affairs. no 10:4-5. Ja. '57.

Verrill, A. H. American Indian. 485p. Appleton. New York. '27.

Verrill, A. H. Real Americans. 309p. G. P. Putnam's Sons. New York. '54.

Wissler, Clark. American Indian: an introduction to the anthropology of the New World. 3d ed. 466p. Oxford University Press. New York. '38.

Wissler, Clark. Indian cavalcade. 370p. Sheridan House. New York. '38.

Wissler, Clark. Indians of the United States. 319p. Doubleday and Co. New York. '40.

PERIODICALS

*American Anthropologist. 56:388-94. Je. '54. American Indian in transition. John Provinse and others.

American Association of University Women Journal. 48:199-203. My. '55. Quick look at Indian affairs today. G. L. Emmons.

American Forests. 60:24-7+. D. '54. Will the Indian make the grade? J. P. Kinney.

American Forests. 61:24-6. S. '55. New hope for the Apache. Charles Cooper.

*American Heritage. 7:5-9+. O. '56. Myths that hide the American Indian. Oliver La Farge.

American Indian (Association on American Indian Affairs). 1:3-11. Summer '44. Justice for the Alaska Indians. Eugene Kelly.

*American Indian (Association on American Indian Affairs). 1:12-22. Summer '44. Indians are citizens. F. S. Cohen.
    Also separate. 4p. mimeo. The Association. 48 E. 86th St. New York 28. '44.

*American Indian (Association on American Indian Affairs). 2:3-11. Spring '45. Indian claims. F. S. Cohen.

*American Indian (Association on American Indian Affairs). 7:1-4. Spring '56. This way lies freedom; statement of policy of the American Association on Indian Affairs.

American Journal of Sociology. 53:17-22. Jl. '47. White pressures on Indian personality. L. M. Thompson and Alice Joseph.

American Magazine. 149:36-7+. Ja. '50. How we scalp the Indians. D. H. Eddy.

American Mercury. 83:132-6. D. '56. Navajo wind that speaks; radio program for Indians. Oren Arnold.

American Scholar. 21, no2:177-9. Spring '52. Americanizing the white man. F. S. Cohen.
    Same condensed. Science Digest. 31:9-13. Je. '52.

*Américas. 6:8-11+. Mr. '54. U.S. Indian speaks. D'Arcy McNickle.

Annals of the American Academy of Political and Social Science. 311:1-165. My. '57. American Indians and American life; ed. by G. E. Simpson and J. M. Yinger.

Arizona Highways. 32:8-13+. S. '56. John Clum, agent unafraid. Lee Stohlbrost.
　　　Reply. 32:40. N. '56. W. T. Corbusier.

Atlantic Monthly. 170:75-81. S. '42. Indians come alive; new hope for native Americans. John Collier.

*Atlantic Monthly. 197:54-7. Mr. '56. Uprooting the Indians; Los Angeles Indian center. R. M. Harmer.
　　　Discussion. 197:20+. Je. '56.

Atlantic Monthly. 199:55-9. F. '57. Cloud of mistrust. E. R. Mirrielees.

*Catholic World. 181:246-51. Jl. '55. Future of the American Indian. T. E. Connolly.

Christian Century. 61:397-8. Mr. 29, '44. Wardship and the Indian. O. G. Villard.

Christian Century. 71:578-80. My. 12, '54. Back to dishonor? John Collier.

*Christian Century. 72:265-7. Mr. 2, '55. Indian winter. H. E. Fey.
　　　Reprinted in Indian rights and American justice. 24p. Christian Century Foundation. 407 South Dearborn St. Chicago 5. '55.

Christian Century. 72:297-9. Mr. 9, '55. Indian and the law. H. E. Fey.

Christian Century. 72:361-4. Mr. 23, '55. Our neighbor the Indian. H. E. Fey.

Christian Century. 72:395-7. Mr. 30, '55. Our national Indian policy. H. E. Fey.

Christian Century. 72:592-4. My. 18, '55. Most Indians are poor. H. E. Fey.

Christian Century. 72:617-9. My. 25, '55. Navajo race with tragedy. H. E. Fey.

Christian Century. 72:680-2. Je. 8, '55. Cherokee trail of tears. H. E. Fey.

Christian Century. 72:728-30. Je. 22, '55. Church and the Indian. H. E. Fey.

Christian Century. 72:835-6. Jl. 20, '55. Are Indians to lose all their land?

Christian Century. 72:1294-6. N. 9, '55. How to help the Indians.

*Christian Century. 73:103-4. Ja. 25, '56. Consultation or consent?

Christian Century. 73:236-8. F. 22, '56. Why care about Indians? H. E. Fey.

Christian Century. 73:476. Ap. 18, '56. Congress should revise our Indian policy.

Christian Century. 73:560-1. My. 2, '56. Seek way to counter Indians' drinking, delinquency. H. L. Lunger.

Christian Century. 73:882-4. Jl. 25, '56. Question validity of Klamath
plan in Oregon. M. A. Talney.
      Reply. 73:1027. S. 5, '56. W. A. Zimmerman, Jr.
Christian Century. 74:227-9. F. 20, '57. It's almost never too late.
D'Arcy McNickle.
Commonweal. 47:510-14. Mr. 5, '48. Americans: with reservations.
M. R. Carse.
Commonweal. 58:505. Ag. 28, '53. New Indian laws.
      Reply. 59:620. O. 23, '53. Ammon Hennacy.
*Coronet. 38:74-6. O. '55. New deal for America's Indians. Madelon
Golden and Lucia Carter.
*Editorial Research Reports. 1, no20:381-98. My. 26, '54. Changing
status of American Indians. H. B. Shaffer.
Freeman. 4:49-51. O. 19, '53. Neither free nor equal. A. L. Tandy
Jemison.
*Harper's Magazine. 212:48-53. Mr. '56. Raid on the reservations.
Dorothy Van de Mark.
      Also separate. 7p. National Congress of American Indians. 1346 Con-
necticut Ave. Washington 6, D.C. '56.
      Discussion. Harper's Magazine. 212:4+. My. '56. 212:8. Jl. '56.
*Harvard Law Record. 22:2-6. Ap. 5, '56. American Indians: people
without a future. Ralph Nader.
      Also separate. 4p. National Congress of American Indians. 1346 Con-
necticut Ave. Washington 6, D.C. '56.
Human Organization. 8, no2:11-14. Spring; no3:25-6. Summer '49.
Indian Bureau and self-government. J. F. Embree.
Human Organization. 11, no4:27-32. Winter '52. Southern Ute re-
habilitation planning; a study in self-determination. R. C. Euler
and H. L. Naylor.
*Indian Affairs (Association on American Indian Affairs). no 14.
F. '56. News letter.
*Indian Affairs (Association on American Indian Affairs). no 15:
supplement. Mr. '56. News letter.
Indian Affairs (Association on American Indian Affairs). no 16.
My.-Je. '56. News letter.
*Indian Affairs (Association on American Indian Affairs). no 18:
supplement. S.-O. '56. Indian legislation in the 84th Congress.
*Indian Affairs (Association on American Indian Affairs). no 19.
Ja. '57. News letter.
      Reprinted in this book: Vanishing homeland. W. O. Roberts. p3-4;
Legislative program for American Indians. p4-5; Administrative program for
American Indians. p5-6.
Indian Truth (Indian Rights Association). p 1-5. Ja.-F. '53. Ameri-
can Indian in tomorrow's America. Charles Russell.
Indian Truth (Indian Rights Association). p 1-3. Mr.-My. '54. In-
dians oppose hasty termination of Federal trusteeship.
Indian Truth (Indian Rights Association). p 1-8. Ap.-Jl. '55. Indian
land holdings threatened.

Indian Truth (Indian Rights Association). p8. Ja.-F. '56. Our American Indian neighbors. H. E. Fey.

Journal of Negro Education. 20, no3:290-300. '51. America's disadvantaged minorities: the American Indian. R. A. Schermerhorn.

Journal of Social Order. 5:57-63. F. '55. Termination in 83d Congress. Lee Metcalf.

Journal of Social Order. 5:64-6. F. '55. City and reservation Indians. George Engstrom and Sister Providencia.

*Journal of Social Order. 5:66-8. F. '55. Obligation of the Federal trust. J. J. Flaherty.

    Also separate with title: Threat to American Indians. 12p. National Congress of American Indians. 1346 Connecticut Ave. Washington 6, D.C. '55.

Look. 19:32-7. Ap. 19, '55. Their plight is our worst disgrace.

*Minnesota Law Review. 24:145-200. '40. Indian rights and the Federal courts. F. S. Cohen.

Nation. 176:29-30. Ja. 10, '53. Letter to General Eisenhower. John Collier.

*Nation. 179:290-1. O. 2, '54. Indian takeaway. John Collier.

National Council Outlook. 5:9+. Ap. '55. Illusion of inability; problems of American Indians. E. R. Carter.

National Council Outlook. 5:17-18. F. '55. Extra friendliness for Indians.

*Nation's Business. 43:40-3+. Jl. '55. U.S. aim: give Indians a chance. G. L. Emmons.

New Mexico Business. p2-8. N. '54. Gallup merchants like it—when Indians come to town. F. M. Sears.

*New York Times. p E-8. F. 24, '57. Beam in our own eye.

New York Times Magazine. p 14-15+. Je. 27, '48. Plea for a square deal for the Indians. Oliver La Farge.

Newsweek. 48:75-6. N. 19, '56. Sioux don't give up.

Reader's Digest. 47:47-52. Ag. '45. Set the American Indians free! O. K. Armstrong.

Reader's Digest. 52:129-32. Ap. '48. Let's give the Indians back to the country. O. K. Armstrong.

*Reader's Digest. 66:39-43. Ja. '55. Indians are going to town. O. K. Armstrong and Marjorie Armstrong.

*Reader's Digest. 67:101-5. N. '55. Give the Indians an even chance. O. K. Armstrong.

Reader's Digest. 70:164-7. Mr. '57. He's giving the Indians a chance. James Daniel.

*Rotarian. 85:26-9. Ag. '54. Whither the American Indian? symposium.

Saturday Evening Post. 217:82. S. 9, '44. Promise that lasted a century. D. McCarty.

Saturday Evening Post. 225:30+. S. 6, '52. These Indians struck it rich; Utes' treaty lands. John Kobler.

*Saturday Evening Post. 227:10+. Jl. 31, '54. Do the Indians want to be free?

Saturday Review. 39:9-10+. S. 22, '56. Suppose Columbus had stayed home. Clyde Kluckhohn.

Saturday Review. 39:24. O. 13, '56. Redskins and U.S. Oliver La Farge.

Science Digest. 22:53-7. N. '47. Indian comes back. J. A. Menaugh.

Senior Scholastic. 51:7-8. Ja. 19, '48. S.O.S. from the American Indians.

Senior Scholastic. 59:12-13. D. 5, '51. Red man's burden.

Senior Scholastic. 62:5-6. Mr. 4, '53. First Americans are last; pro and con discussion.

Social Service Review. 27:214. Je. '53. Indians are full-fledged citizens.

Social Service Review. 27:193-200. Je. '53. Indian administration: problems and goals. D. S. Myer.

*Survey Graphic. 29:168-74. Mr. '40. Whither the American Indian? Alden Stevens.

Time. 68:31. S. 17, '56. Ambush.

Travel. 73:18-22+. S. '39. New deal for the American Indian. Harold Ward.

Yale Law Journal. 62:348-90. F. '53. Erosion of Indian rights, 1950-53; a case study in bureaucracy. F. S. Cohen.

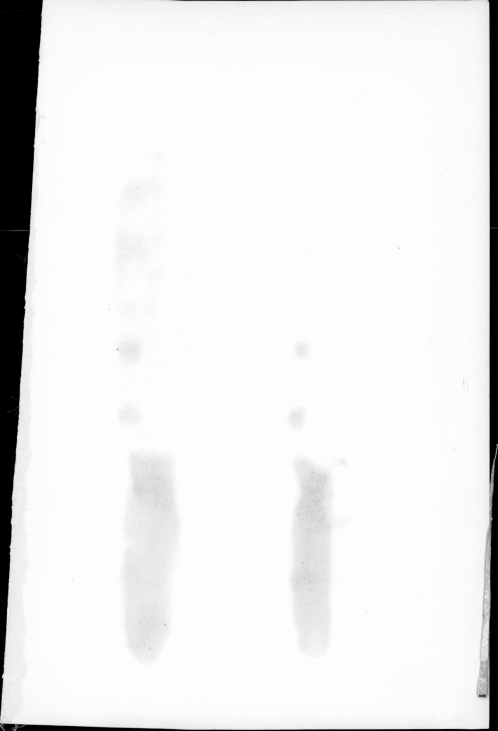